THE POEMS

OF

ROBERT LOWELL,

AUTHOR OF "THE NEW PRIEST IN CONCEPTION BAY."

A NEW EDITION

(WITH MANY NEW POEMS.)

BOSTON:
E. P. DUTTON AND COMPANY.
1864.

RIVERSIDE, CAMBRIDGE:
STEREOTYPED AND PRINTED BY H. O. HOUGHTON.

To

JOSEPH GREEN COGSWELL, LL. D.,

THE FIRST HEAD OF ROUND-HILL SCHOOL,

TO WHOM THE BOY BROUGHT HIS LESSONS WITH MUCH
REVERENCE AND LOVE AND WITHOUT FEAR,
THE MAN OFFERS THIS BOOK AS
FEARLESSLY AND WITH
NO LESS LOVE AND
REVERENCE.

JULY 31, 1863.

HAVING from childhood met, now and then, and listened to the Muse of Numbers, the writer offers here a few of the few things that he has learned, at different times, from her, and hopes that they may not be thought too many.

Lest the dates, put to most of them, should be thought to have been occasioned by a conceit or affectation, it is right to say that they are owing to a friend's discovery of a remarkable chance-likeness between one of these, printed years ago, and a recent poem in a Magazine. One being dated, some others, at least, must be so; and in the end, most of these pieces have had the time at which they were written, given, after them. The general reader will be kind enough to pass over these dates as harmless; some friends may even find a slight interest in them.*

* Some persons may need to be told that, where more than one date is given, the piece was left (forgotten, perhaps) altogether, between; then found and carried on.

March, 1860.

CONTENTS.

AN ANTHEM-CAROL FOR CHRISTMAS.

Out of highest heaven dropping,
Like tinkling rain upon the sea
Came sweet music, swelling, stopping;
'Twas the angels' symphony.
"Glory be to God, on high!"
Ran like lightning round the sky:
Then, like rain-drops, fell agen,
"Peace on earth, good-will to men!"

1846.

This little tragedy shaped itself in my mind from the suggestion of two or three words in a note to a Greek Author, as I remembered them, afterwards; a poem "by a boy" (without a name) was mentioned as having come down from earlier times. The Reader is to set the time three thousand years back.*

* The Title is an earlier (and shorter) one than that with which it was first printed: the Poem is the same.

THE DELPHIAN CHILDREN

AND THEIR LOST HOPE.

I.

A YOUTH lay near the fair gulf's* fringéd shore;
The noise of Corinth scarcely came so far;
But landward sounds, that, when the day is o'er,
Tell where blest homes and ended labors are.
On the broad bay, behind,
Lugged by the lazy wind,
A freighted ship drew on, towards the evening-
star.

II.

The little waters, as the daylight waned,
Lagged up the beach, prattling with shell and
stone;

* Of Corinth.

The eastern sky was all with sunset stained,
Where the two heads of that great mountain *
shone.
Lower, each vale and glade
Drew in, to deeper shade,
The eye of him that gazed from that far shore
alone.

III.

Still lay, bright-hued, in air, both far and
wide,
All crumbled rays the sun had thrown away;
And, floating thick on the night's dewy tide,
Came smells more sweet than scents of burn-
ing day;
And then a voice, — as fair
As all the best things there, —
Scarce startling him; old, gentle, sweet, and
sad as they: —

IV.

"Thou musest of the gifts that, yonder, wait
Those whom the Gods do choose with far-off
ken:

* Mount Parnassus.

Castalia's spell,* and the rich, dreamy freight
Laid on Sleep's shore,† for favored sons of men.
I sought one sacred gift: —
Ah! Time's waves, strong and swift,
Have swept bright looks and hopes, that made
my world glad, then.

V.

"Beside a pool, where, still, two olives meet,
Threescore years since, some Delphian ‡ children played:
We built our little mole and launched our fleet,
And then along the rippling margin strayed
Watching the voyage o'er,
Till, at the farther shore,
Our galleys, one by one, on the safe strand
were laid.

VI.

"Mine, ever mine, was foremost in the race,
Till, tired, our little maidens sat them down,

* Whoever drank of the water, might drink the divine spirit also.

† He that slept upon Parnassus, in waking found his mind possessed by poetic inspiration, or was possessed by madness.

‡ The city of Delphi, where was the great temple of Apollo, stood upon the mountain, a mile or more from the foot.

Whispered apart, — then sang: — one, with
bright face,
Said, 'Let our poet wear a Pythian crown!'
They wove the dark-leaved beech,
Each helping, hindering each,
Then, in child's triumph, all turned homeward
to the town.

VII.

"On huge Parnassus hung a wondrous cloud, —
We children marked it, — much like yon fair
show;
Again Alcestis spoke, but scarce aloud,
'At times the mighty Shades do gather so.
(So did my mother say;)
They come not in the day,
But in still night, to walk the high woods to
and fro:'

VIII.

"Shades of the great old Greeks and Barbarous men,
Whoe'er on earth had loosed some mighty song:
At times by night they wandered here, and
then
What poet found the haunt of the dread throng

On that far mountain-height,
Ere dawn was lost in light,
That once, plucked fadeless flowers that to their
realm belong.

IX.

"My heart beat quickly, as we gazed and walked,
For they had all praised my own childish
rhyme;
Evadne, too, my sister, while we talked,
Turned her full eyes, as if I, child, might climb
Up to that haunted land;
Alcestis pressed my hand
As if she felt my heart throb at the very time.

X.

"I lost our Pythian garland in the road,
While we walked thoughtfully, and sometimes
spake.
The wondrous cloud with the last sunlight
glowed,
As yon cloud lately: — might not we awake, —
We three, — from early rest,
And on the mountain's breast,
Climb with fresh, hopeful hearts, high ere the
day could break?

XI.

"Out of glad day, through the fair porch of eve,
Our playmates passed into the halls of sleep.
I listened long, for the great town to leave
Its noise and watchfulness, and long rest keep.
Then faltered forth, to gain
The great god's awful fane,
Scared by each far, lone cry, and the far, conscious deep.

XII.

"I shrank before the columns cloaked with shade,
And, shuddering, felt a fanning of great wings:
I dared not that chill presence to invade,
Dim with dread forms of gods and godlike kings.
I gasped my childish prayer:
I had no garland there
To offer, as men vow their gifts and glorious things.

XIII.

"Ere that fair night had reached her highest bound,
We met and grasped each other's trembling hand;

With faltering whispers scaled the fearful ground,
Three children where dread rocks and huge trees
stand.
On high the broad moon rolled;
And her rays, white and cold,
From darkness, here and there, scarce won the
doubtful land.

XIV.

"We kept a torrent's course, and, trembling
still,
Went on and on, starting and stopping oft:
Sometimes we sat and wept, as children will,
And my cheek felt Evadne's, wet and soft:
'Home!' she would gently say,
"Nay!' said Alcestis, 'nay!'
And still we clambered on, through the dread
woods, aloft.

XV.

"Hours, hours went on, and cold and darkness
grew:
Still, weary and afraid, we clambered fast,
And dawn began to gray the night's deep blue:
We gained the upper woods! — The way was
past!

Now need we only seek
Where the two echoes speak,
Above, below, at once, to find the flowers that
last.

XVI.

"Our voices faltered, when we strove to sing:
We feared the trees, the rocks, the quivering
gloom:
At length we dared our little hymn to fling
Through the thin air, where shadowy horrors
loom.
Lo! at the earliest sound,
The mystic spot was found,
And there a high, smooth cliff, crowned with
undying bloom.

XVII.

"Great characters upon the rock's high face
Slowly we saw, in the dim dawning light;
'MEN THAT WERE MAKERS,'* far up we could
trace,
And then their names that had the Maker's
might;

* 'ΑΝΔΡΕΣ ΠΟΙΗΤΑΙ' it may be read.

We thought not what great hand
Had made those names to stand:
We thought that at the foot a boy's name we
might write.

XVIII.

" So, with weak hand, I sought to print the
stone,
The little maidens sitting at my side.
'First,' said Alcestis, 'make the flowers thine
own!'
'Nay,' said Evadne, with a sister's pride,
'Let our young poet's name
Stand on this roll of fame!'
So I, with hurrying hand, my weary labor
plied.

XIX.

" Slowly the dawning grew, and slowly I
Now wrought, now rested; but Alcestis still
Said, 'Gather first the blooms that hang on high!
Day will be here ere thou this task fulfil:
Yon peak sees it afar,
And yonder shrinking star;
First gain the fadeless flowers, then work here
at thy will.'

XX.

" Four letters rudely in the stone were wrought,
And could be read, 'A Boy,' * but yet no name.
'See,' said Alcestis, 'how the peak has caught
Already daylight: soon 't will be a-flame.
It is not yet too late!
Mount where the bright flowers wait:
Flowers that, when thou art dead, will ever be
the same!'

XXI.

" I tried the cliff, and climbed: my hands were
sore,
And I was tired: yet I strained up the height.
The little maidens shouted, 'Yet once more!'
I tried: I tried: I could not reach them quite.
And ah! behold on high,
Ah! all across the sky,
The day was come, at last, and *dawn was lost
in light.*

XXII.

" My tears burst forth: in vain my sister said,
'They are still there!' — I knew it was in vain.

* 'ΠΑΙΣ' — but as yet no name, *it may be read.*

It was too late. — Alcestis hung her head.
Sadly I came down to the earth, again.
'Home!' said Alcestis, now:
Evadne kissed my brow;
And, by our torrent's course, we toiled down
to the plain."

The little waters trickled down the beach,
And landward sounds fell, faintly, to their rest.
The dews were heavy, and that sad, soft speech
Had ceased, just when the ear had liked it
best.
The young man was alone,
And great cool night was thrown
Over wide earth and sea, from far east to far
west.

June 16–20, 1858.

A HOUSE ON THE YELLOW SAND.

I BUILT a house on the golden sand,
With the gleamy sea beside;
It looked forth, here, on the dear, loved land,
And there on the changing tide.

It was sweet spring-time, and the days all fair,
Till the pretty work was done;
And the house seemed akin to the bright, clear air,
And the summer glance of the sun.

But a wind with waves came up from the sea,
And burst through the weak shore's check;
They spoiled all my pleasant things for me,
And my house was all a wreck.

The seasons changed, and the strong land-wind
Drove back all my fickle sand;
But only a waste was left behind,
And my walls no longer stand.

Trust not the golden, yellow sand,
  The sea, nor the changeful blast;
Dig deep in the strength of the fast-set land,
  And thy home shall stand as fast.

1860.

THE WARNED ONE.

SILENT watcher, see'st thou aught
On the far-off ocean's brim?
Has thine eye a meaning caught
In the mist-world's changeful whim?
Gaze full long, and gaze full deep:
There is that which chaseth sleep
In the spirit-forms that rise
Far before thy fated eyes.
Be thou, watcher, timely wise.

Blessed are those sons of men
For whose sake a light is set
Out beside things far-off, yet,
So to bring them within ken;
Showing them in ghastly white,
While beyond is depth of night:
Blessed are they, if they know
What these things far-moving are,
Coming, coming, sure if slow,
They give warning, thus, afar.

July, 1847.

THE DAYS OF SIN.

OH, mournful, mournful time!
  I prayed: but sin was there:
  Sin crept upon my prayer,
And made my prayer a crime!

I prayed, and prayed again:
  But sin was in it still!
  It throttled my weak will;
I struggled — but in vain.

I burned by day and night,
  I feared that fire of sin —
  Its covering seemed so thin —
Would show to other's sight!

My daily work I did, —
  I talked of Heaven and Hell,
  Full often and full well, —
But ah! what woe I hid!

It seemed as if my fate
  Were up: in Satan's mesh —
  A damnéd soul in flesh —
I lived beyond my date.

Christ's life in me seemed lost!
  Where was the promise now,
  Sealed to me when my brow
In his blest sign was cross'd?

I strove to fly from me;
  Always it was the same;
  Hell was where'er I came;
God's wrath I could not flee.

Such life I loathed to keep,
  But could I dare to die?
  Heaven's walls so hopeless high
And Hell a soundless deep?

My heart aye told me well
  I gave myself away,
  To be the Devil's prey —
By my own hand I fell.

I struggled once for all;
  God's altar — there I prayed;

  And bitter cry I made
Behind my closet wall.

A change began to be!
  I felt the Breath of Life!
  For Heaven and Hell was strife:
I struggled, and was free!

Ah! now the strife was done:
  I sought the Flesh and Blood;
  I ate Salvation's food;
My soul to Christ was won.

February 10, 1847.

THE LITTLE YEARS.

A SONG FOR THE ELDER GRADUATES.

THESE years! These years! These naughty
years
Once they were pretty things:
Their fairy foot-falls caught our ears,
Our eyes their glancing wings.
They flitted by our school-boy way;
We chased the little imps at play.

We knew them, soon, for tricksy elves;
They brought the college gown;
With thoughtful books filled up our shelves,
Darkened our lips with down:
Played with our throat, and lo! the tone
Of manhood had become our own.

They smiling stretched our childish size;
Their soft hands trimmed our hair;
Cast the deep thought within our eyes
And left it glowing there:

Sang songs of hope in college-halls,
Bright fancies drew upon the walls.

They flashed upon us love's bright gem;
They showed us gleams of fame;
Stout-hearted work we learned from them,
And honor more than name:
And so they came and went away,
We said not go: we said not stay.

But one sweet day, when quiet skies
And still leaves brought me thought,
When hazy hills drew forth my eyes,
And woods with deep shade fraught,
That day I carelessly found out
What work these elves had been about.

Alas! Those little rogues, the years,
Had fooled me many a day;
Plucked half the locks above my ears,
And tinged the rest all gray.
They'd left me wrinkles, great and small:—
I fear that they have tricked us all.

Well,—give the little years their way;
Think, speak, and act, the while:

Lift up the bare front to the day,
And make their wrinkles smile:
They mould the noblest living head;
They carve the best tomb for the dead.

July 20, 1858.

[Hands skilful and famous have taken this up to make a tune for it; and yet it wants one, that it may be, as was meant, and as the maker longs to have it, sung by the Elder Graduates.]

OUR INLAND SUMMER-NIGHTFALL.

WITHIN the twilight came forth tender snatches
Of birds' songs from beneath their darkened
eaves:
But now a noise of poor ground-dwellers matches
This dimness: neither loves, nor joys, nor grieves.
A piping, slight and shrill,
And coarse, dull chirpings fill
The ear that all day's stronger, finer music leaves.

From this smooth hill, we see the vale below,
there,
And how the mists along the stream-course
draw:
By day, great trees from other ages grow there,
A white lake, now, that daylight never saw.
It hugs, in ghostly shape,
The Old Deep's shore and cape,

As when, where night-hawks skim, swam fish
with yawning maw. *

All grows more cool, though night comes slowly over,
And slowly stars stand out within the sky!
The trampling market-herd and way-sore drover
Crowd past with seldom cries, — their halt now nigh.
From out some lower dark
Comes up a dog's short bark:
There food and welcome rest, there cool, soft meadows lie.

The children, watching by the roadside wicket,
Now houseward troop, for Blindman's-Buff, or Tag;
Here chasing sidelong, fire-flies to the thicket,
There shouting, with a grass-tuft reared for flag.
They claim this hour from night:
But with a sure, still sleight,
The sleep-time clogs their feet, and one by one they lag.

* In our narrower, deep dells and valleys, the mist will hide, altogether, the trees, and show how, in old times, the great waters filled all these deep places.

Our doctor jogs, with loose rein, on the highway,
Near where the lawyer with his rake is set:
Short greeting, — and the two, in merry, sly way,
Tease with old jokes that have their fresh-
ness, yet.
This charges clients lost:
That, law's most hopeless cost,
And heart-strain that by healing-skill is never
met.

A farmer, with his coat across his shoulder,
Leans, with his youngest boy in arms, to wait
While, with big words, and oft-jerked reins,
the older
Urges the unhitched horses through the gate.
A little girl, unshod,
Stands by with idle rod,
Her sweet-breathed cows long since brought
home with welcome freight.

Far down the road faint shouts of maidens'
laughter
Mark twilight-meeting by the open well:
Now stillness for some tale; gainsayings, after,
Prove, shrilly, how well-thrown some youth's
name fell.

Not only maidens hear:
A sudden rougher jeer
Makes known some ambushed ears and tongues the tale to tell.

Things have not kindly ties, within a city;
Here thoughts hang garlanded on wayside trees,
Where Will made endless mirth, Hal sang his ditty:
One fell in our great war: one sails far seas:
And here, at some smooth stone,
Have young hearts often known
That lordly bondage, first, that first the young heart frees.

Dusk arms our moral taverner with drenches
More safe for sots that now no longer taste;
While slow-tongued neighbors fill his outer benches,
For these still hours, their evening reek to waste.
Squire, here, and stroller meet;
And yet one empty seat
Awaits the greater man, or else is left in haste.

All know of all, and dwellings, roads, and bridges;

The crop's best hope, fresh colts, and horses
lame;
Tell what a Father thought on drills and
ridges,
Name children, sick, and the last guest that
came.
An easy common-law
Holds party strifes in awe;
Our fiery smith, alone, his rash tongue scarce
can tame.

In one far cot a clarinet is droning;
Lads strive in whistling on the southern hill;
The farness and the dew-soft air atoning
For noise so kept alive with tireless will.
Who sighs for rich and proud,
The great Town's nightly crowd,
Its song, its show, its sin, their harmless place
to fill?

From our priest's household, as the night draws
nearer,
Through windows open pours a holy song,
Sung to their own hearts and One Kindest
Hearer, —

For many a child's note wanders freely wrong.
Yet is the sound most meet,
With day far under feet,
And dimness here, and sleep, — for all to God
belong.

And now the still stars make all heaven sightly;
One, in the low west, like the sky ablaze:
The Swan, that with her shining Cross floats
nightly,
And Bears that slowly walk along their ways.
There is the golden Lyre,
And there the Crown of fire:
Thank God for nights so fair to these bright
days!

[Written as it happened, during the days of the base riots in New York City, July, 1863.]

A CHRISTMAS HYMN.

THE first time that the skies grew bright,
  When Heaven lay open wide,
And angels gleamed adown the night
  Of one still country-side;

'Twas when the Almighty Heir of All
  Came forth, a helpless child,
Amid the darkness of a stall,
  And through our nature smiled.

Far down in Being, but forgot
  By none who watched afar,
Above the lowly, hidden spot
  Was buoyed one floating star.

Then angels, up the heights of sky,
  Flashed glory with their shout,
And o'er the wide earth sleeping nigh,
  Fell words of peace about.

TURNING LOVE AWAY.

(LONG YEARS AGO.)

O LOVE, go forth! I brought thee here
For that I heard thee sing one day
When thou wast in the grass at play:
That song of one that was too dear.
O Love! — O Love! — I could not bear
To listen by the wayside there;
I longed to hear thee sing, somewhere
Where no one else was near.

Rememberest thou, my little guest?
In bearing thee, (thy pretty wing
Blinding my eyes, thou roguish thing!)
I wandered where my feet knew best.
She laid on thee a timid touch,
But oh! that little was so much,
The arrows in thy careless clutch
Stung all my open breast.

How bright the earth was, that glad time!
How sweetly breathed the evening air;
It seemed her breath was everywhere,
And ours became a fairy clime!
The sky hung all in gold and red;
The flowers all vied their scents to shed;
The ground seemed loving to my tread;
All sounds, that eve, did chime.

I gave thee but one only task:
To go as my true messenger,
And bring sweet words again from her,
The work thyself didst ask:
Until that day between us two
Thou broughtest lies; we thought them true,
So well our cunning traitor knew
His young, false face to mask.

I must shut up thy little room! —
Ah! o'er its yet unhardened wall
Thine arrow traced her name, and all
Her look, except her own fresh bloom! —
I could not come here but to weep:
Here was thy little couch to sleep;
These walls thy useless work will keep;
But this shall be a tomb.

Let me forget that lying tongue!
Ah, what a price its falsehood cost,
When once, was once forever, lost! —
Yet sleep that loss, lost things among!
For such this world makes no amends.
We drew apart and chose new friends:
So many a short, bright story ends,
Where two young hearts were wrung.

A WALK AMONG MEMORY'S GRAVES.

I.

GRAVES of the silent dead,
Ye echo to the tread
Of a lone, mourning man:
They were my friends of yore;
Sweet company they bore
To me when life began.

II.

I wander here, alone,
To seek if faithful stone
Is set by every grave;
And to call up again
Thoughts, cherished not in vain,
They to my young soul gave.

III.

Yours first I call, dear Hopes,
Seen on the sunny slopes,

Where as a child I lay;
Or that by winding brook,
My loitering steps o'ertook,
In the long summer day.

IV.

There was no sound of man;
My free soul forward ran
Among the coming years.
I felt the breath of fame:
I heard aloud my name:
My eyes were nigh to tears.

V.

Glad Hopes! Ye gave me then
What long, late toil to men
Brings only withering:
I plucked with childish gripe,
The fruit ere it was ripe;
But it was mine in spring.

VI.

Sweet, sweet, sad Hopes! what now
Is left upon the bough,
Of flower, or fruit, or leaf?
And yet, why mourn, if ye

So early gave to me
Thoughts fair and bright, though brief?

VII.

Feelings of childhood's time,
That stretched about to climb
On all that stood around!
Whose twining grasp was laid,
In sunshine and in shade,
Tireless on all it found, —

VIII.

Whose hold was often flung
From that whereon ye clung,
Yet would not long be free;
By your fond instinct taught
I thought (true childhood's thought)
That all were kin to me.

IX.

Amid the boys' loud band
I seem again to stand;
Again quick-voiced and glad;
Feelings more great and strong
Than to child's sports belong
In those young days we had:

X.

The swell, ere storms begin,
When huge waves tumble in
And fill the little bay;
So from life's vexéd sea,
The strong, deep swell knew we,
In childhood's peaceful day.

XI.

That human brotherhood,
Mingling in every mood,
Made this our life so great,
The mystic, awful bond
Still urged me forth beyond
Myself, to feel my fate:

XII.

One of so many more,
Whom life was laid before
Full of mysterious things;
Where every human soul,
To the great common whole,
Its lore and insight brings.

XIII.

I look once more to see,
As at the chestnut tree

Where the far voices died,
The pleasant thoughts that played
Beneath that pleasant shade,
In troops on every side.

XIV.

Then youth came sailing o'er,
Fairer than all before,
Broad-sailed and deeply fraught.
Love! Hope! Ambition! you
Mastered the lithe, strong crew.—
Love?—Hope?—Ambition?—Naught!

XV.

Yet, if they were but vain,
They come no more again
To make me loiter here:
The work that God has set,
It has the long days, yet,
And brightest of the year.

XVI.

Still has my chief work been
Rather to make me clean,
As he must be that will
Go forth 'mid thronging men

And stretch his forward ken
Onward and upward, still.
* * * * * *

XVII.

No more, no more I call!
Cool, solemn shadows fall
Down on my open mind!
For this I wandered here —
For this I called you near,
Thoughts of things long resigned;

XVIII.

They will be raised one day,
And throng about the way
Of the old dying man;
Hopes, feelings, joys that smiled
Upon him when a child,
And o'er the bright scenes ran.

XIX.

Children in summer's eve,
Do pluck the old man's sleeve
And clamber up his knee;
Or draw him by the hand
To where their playthings stand,
Or their sweet sports to see.

XX.

Thus will these come, once more,
To lead him gently o'er
The scenes loved long ago;
And in his eldest days,
All childhood's long left ways
Make him again to know.

July, 1846.

[One stanza was put in and the neighboring parts adjusted to it in 1860.]

A DREAM OF JUDGMENT JUST AT HAND.

THE Earth doth rock! the Earth doth reel!
It topples like a poiséd wheel,
When the hand that held it falls.
Its burning heart doth throb with dread,
As the mighty blast both quick and dead
Forth to God's Judgment calls.
The shattered air is drowned in rain:
No cloud shall ever come again.
The leaves hang down: the rank grass droops:
The storm-unshaken mountain stoops;
The ocean's roar is heard:
Less! less! and less! Ah, it doth cease!
Its broad, smooth bosom waits in peace
For the Almighty Word.
* * * * *
Earth is riven! Rocks are rent!
Darting flames are upwards sent:
Everywhere the fire has vent:
Every sepulchre is burst:
Dust from dust, dust from dust,

Lo! the sinner and the just, —
To be blessed, to be blessed, blessed, or forever
curst.

Crowding, crowding, they are cóme,
Millions, countless, yet is room,
Though each sod has been a tomb.
On the waters millions stand,
Still, as those on fixéd land.
Not a whisper, — not a breath; —
They have not yet unlearned death.
Pale, pale, oh, ghastly pale!
And the thin bodies are no more a veil
To the souls that are within,
They are so sere and thin.

Wretched, oh, wretched, wretched sight!
Every secret brought to light.
Tongue could not speak, hand could not write.
* * * * * * *
The sun! the sun!
The end of all things is begun.
How near! how bright!
But oh, the Earth
What is its beauty worth! what are its riches
worth!

What are its paltry glories worth!
'Tis of too small a girth,—this despicable earth,—
For the Last Deed that yet is to be done.

Speech! Human speech? No! 'tis not human
speech!
That tone no voice of man could reach!
'Tis a new sound on earth, — a screech
Of the Doomed Dead raised up:
Lord God, oh, how it doth beseech
But for one chance, a single chance, but one!

Voices, voices, everywhere,
Hiss and hurtle in the heavy air.
The air is dead: no more they breathe:
The air is dead, above, beneath.

Oh, what voices crowd mine ear!
All that ever died are here,
And God's great, last Doom so near!
All life, now, seems only fear!
All at once, yet separate,
I hear them all: each has its date
And following: Time is not done,
And yet Eternity almost begun:
Eternity and Time just blending into one.

Oh! oh! how soon, how soon shall this last
time be done!
Hark! a dull, thick earthly tongue,
And still with thought all earthly hung:
"Help me to pile this costly stone
Above my neighbor: — 'twas my own: —
Nay, nay, nay, nay; — let all alone;
He is not there: but can I yet atone? ——
My heart was never in that wrong:
Fate drives men's blinded wills along:
I strove; but I was weak, and it was strong.
Thou dost not blame? Kneel with me, then,
And hide this shame from God and men.
This long, carved lie, that time forgot,
For Christ's sake, help me here to blot:
Help me! — thou dost not fear thy lot."
* * * * * * *

There is a sound of preparation heard,
For the dread coming of the Heavenly King,
As when the deep wood-depths unseen are stirred
Ere with the tempest's mighty gust they swing.
The King is coming: He that long ago
Came to this earth, a Man of woman born,
And o'er its wide face wandered to and fro,
Weary and weeping, and with travel worn,
Eating with earth's most wretched and forlorn. —

A fair light flares upon the sky, as if before the
morn.

* * * * * * * *

Here are fair things: if women, or if men,
The eye scarce marks; and yet the heart may
know
That these were wedded, and unsundered, when
Death into want and waste their flesh brought
low.
Here is no fondness; here is no desire:
But one kind likeness grown where love filled all;
And here is mother's-love that could not tire
Nor be put off; and manly heart's true fire
That gave up all his own at others' call.
Now all is upward cast, and onward longs:
Christ is the lovely One, to whom all turn.
Onward to Him the holy feeling throngs,
And love that learned of Him, to Him doth yearn.

* * * * * * * *

What desperate voice crawls upward from the dust?
What thing lies here, without all love, faith, hope
and trust?
I am no king:
I am some meanest thing,
That washes beggars' feet: — I seek no throne,
I can bear always to be trod upon.

They that for me in sudden graves have lain, —
Must I forever wear a guilty stain?
Death never was to last:
Who sleeps, since that dread trumpet-blast?"

Onward and upward glows the conquering light,
Spreading the skies around with gilded white;
And soft sweet sounds of mighty love breathe out,
Strewing the Saviour's path with heavenly flowers
about.
He comes, He comes whom every eye shall see!
Lord, all the nations turn their eyes for thee!

* * * * * * * *

Was this man rich? and never rich with love?
Oh, how his cry is strained all sounds above!
"Holy prayers I made;
And countless alms have paid!
I have built churches, and my name was known
Abroad, wherever winds have blown!

"It is on record: was it all for nought?
What price, then, ever, Paradise has bought?
When earth burns, that cheating wealth
Let it drain away by stealth:
Had I given, had I given,
I might lift my eyes to heaven!"

As the wide water spreadeth on the land,
With mighty softness taking every place,
Until the flood alone doth all-wheres stand;
So doth the Presence of the King at hand
In mildest conquest make its way, apace,
Till all is held and mastered in His Grace.

Now, little voices, sweet beyond all sweet,
Pour to the most kind Lord their welcomes fleet.
"Hosanna! Glory in the highest be,
O son of David, loving Lord, to Thee!"

Like some new life, made lightly of soft notes,
This way and that, above, the child-song floats.

He that sat glittering up on high,
But knew not God, oh, what a bitter cry!
"I would kneel before my door,
Calling round the filthy poor, —
I would crawl upon my knees
To the side of loathed disease, —
Worse things, and baser things than these, —
Could I lick the very sore
With distemper running o'er, —
No! no! no! my season is no more!"

* * * * * * *

Soft sound comes forth from them that gird the
Lord
Forever with their band of circling love,
Like and unlike, yet all in blest accord:
Earth hath not heard such sounds since it did
move
At first, to most sweet measure, when the Word
Sent it forth blessèd, and the sons of God
With joyous song timed its far march abroad.
Down, grovelling down, the man of bloody hand
Sinks, while his cheek with those blest sounds is
fanned.
"I thrust God's life out from my brother man:
Now a long death my endless life shall span;
And in the dread strife conquer neither can!"

The bright clouds open: Glory swelleth through;
Millions upon their bended knees do fall:
These shall be saved: these are the chosen few:
Lo! on their brow a cross of glittering dew
Shines with that Glory. These were faithful, all,
And, while they lived, beyond their season small
Saw ever Judgment, Heaven, and Hell, in view:
These followed Christ and listened to His call,
New-born of water and the Holy Ghost;
And, being most forgiven, loved Him most,

Upheld with heavenly food to keep the way,
With living food renewed and strengthened, day
by day.

Falsehood and guile not yet their own place seek:
What words all thick with shame the lips can
speak!
There is no manhood in that deathly cheek. —
"Those are still vows that then I spoke,
Though all that man can break I broke.
I see how strong God's high Word stands:
Yes, though I blind me with my hands!
I broke my oaths, I broke thy heart,
I broke God's law and endless love apart.
He holds me not! — I feel no tie above! —
Nothing my heart knows of Christ's blessèd love.
Child! wilt thou, too, go into bliss
With a fresh memory of this?
This most sad thing, this last of earth,
His doom, to whom thou owest birth?
Is Heaven such? Is Hell so near?
That thou in heaven itself mayest hear
The hopeless shriek, the frightful shout,
That must and ever will burst out,
Ever and ever, from the damnèd rout?
And know 'That is my Father wailing there;

That voice I know?' Despair! Despair!"

* * * * * * * *

Great silence falls: but silence full of sound,
And full of splendor: and the Lord is found,
Here in the midst, at hand, and not afar,
And beauteous living things about Him are.
The eyes that looked on Mary, look on all,
And in our hearts words that men speak not fall:
The very thorns, — the spear-wound and the nails!
Life is become but love, and all thought fails.

1845; finished July, 1863.

A SONG FOR CHRISTMAS.

Carol, Christians! Christ is here!
Carol for this Baby dear!
This is Man, but God, the more;
Sing beside this stable-door!

This our King, without a crown
In a manger is laid down,
Where the Maid, with meekest hands,
Wrapped him all in swathing-bands.

Ages long ago He came,
Lived and died, yet is the same:
He, who, slain ere Things were made,
In this stall a Babe was laid.

Sing, good Christians! come and sing!
Praise our Christ, and praise our King!
Gladdest Night! most happy Morn!
Christ, our Lord, this Day was born!

Sing our best, both Young and Old!
Never heart, this time, be cold!
Never eye of love be dim!
Who love others, they love Him.

THE PAINTER'S PROBATION.

[How he strives to make the fairest painting that was ever made in earth.]

PART FIRST.

THERE comes in life a frequent hour,
When the full voice of Fate
Calls with a dread, mysterious power
On those who should be great:
To warn them that a mighty dower
Somewhere for them doth wait.
For somewhere, in the long, long train
That marches down through Time,
Working out human nature's gain,
Its glory or its crime,
For each a station doth remain:
With power to do or to refrain,
A humble or sublime.
And they whom God hath breathed upon
And gifted, from their birth,

With lofty powers to labor on
The labor of this earth,
For them, amid the swelling crowd,
An office is assigned
With mighty influence endowed;
And unto them Fate calleth, loud,
In the first-opening mind.
Again, again, through shine or cloud,
Her words come, as the wind.
Alas! how many, downward bowed.
Their birthright have resigned!
O God! How much of great and good,
How much of fearful sin,
Were gained, or gallantly withstood,
If these their place would win!

There hung upon the chamber-wall
The fancies he had wrought:
All that his soul had power to call,
Out of the shapes that shadow all,
Into his burning thought.
The hopes that gladdened early years
Had left their colors there,
And shades were there, that early fears

Had taught his art to wear:
Alternate smiles, alternate tears,
(So that young life to thought appears,)
Each memory had its share.
But in the dark and in the bright, —
Colored by joy or pain, —
Something was wanting to his sight:
The utmost all were vain.
Sweet strains of music from old days
Murmured about his soul,
And Memory's deep, golden haze,
An atmosphere of mingled rays,
O'er his wide thought would roll,
While airs, like summer wind that plays,
Would gently fan the whole.
Oh! at such seasons, when he felt
As if his spirit, free
From the close body's narrow belt,
Swelled towards Divinity,
And pure and strong and living grew,
As when at first it came
From Him that sent it forth to do
Deeds that should earn a name,
Or, nameless, bear a blessing through
The paths of this world's shame,
Oh! why, when God himself inspired

Those raptured hours of thought,
The very seasons oft desired,
Why has he yet in vain retired,
And still no trophy brought,
Though, by a transient impulse fired,
Again he strove and wrought?
He saw the scene: he felt the force;
He started forth to do!
But no! the streamlet from its source
Bears flowers of every hue
Wrapped in their seeds; and, in its course,
It strews and plants them too:
But time, and place, and God's own smile
Must meet together, or long while
Unfruitful they must lie,
Ere they will show again the scene
From which they came, and which has been
Painted in many-colored sheen
Beneath another sky.
Thus all were vain: he could not find
Within his utmost power,
That form that floated in his mind,
Not indistinct, though not defined,
Leaving a memory behind,
Like tints at sunset hour.
His gleaming eye had caught its light,

His cheek had felt its glow;
And dreamily before his sight,
In the rapt visions of the night,
That fancy-form would go;
And when his spirit felt its might,
That form he seemed to know.
In the wild agony of prayer
His trembling hand had tried
To fix the fleeting figure there:
And he had sought in mad despair
The power that was denied.
All Beauty and all Holiness, —
(Alas! there mingled Sin,) —
Howe'er combined, could not express
That form he sought to win.
There was the blue of changeless Truth:
There was Love's burning red;
The golden-glowing Hope of Youth
Its yellow glory spread:
Oh, pure! oh, bright! oh, heavenly deep!
There seemed God's Light within,
And wings of angels seemed to sweep
The breathing work: but shades did creep
O'er all: there mingled Sin!
That chill, chill wind from o'er the graves
And from the cold, damp tomb,

That wind that frosts the hair it waves,
And pales the cheek's fresh bloom;
The bitter wind that we must face
As down life's hill we go apace,
And evening spreads its gloom; —
He felt its first cold-creeping breath,
And saw afar, in mist, the vast, dim shape
of Death.

Come down, O night of dreamless sleep!
Come to this sad, sad room:
This working will and spirit steep
In silence, not in gloom.
Be thou, O night of needed rest,
A calm, clear night of peace,
Wherein the voice of heavenly guest
Can sing his gentle soothings best,
That make earth's struggles cease;
And, in the shut and darkened mind,
Leave sweetest lingering notes behind,
That shall the calm increase,
Until with waking prayer they find,
As with a breath of morning wind,
A happy, fit release.
And ye, O flowers of earnest Thought,

That in his mind grew bright,
With fresher perfume shall be fraught
And fairer robes, of spirits caught,
Cast down in peaceful night.

1838 and 1846.

END OF PART FIRST.

[The Author must ask those who are interested to wait for the Second Part of The Painter's Probation. In finishing the First Part, he set up a few lines of the other, to start with: but has not touched them since.]

THAT DEAD.

Is he gone? Oh! Is he gone?
And does the world still travel on,
Heedless of his loss,
Like a freighted ship, at sea,
Ploughing on, though there may be
One that perished suddenly,
In the deep, like dross?

He is dead: yes, he is dead:
Bands of earth bind down his head,
Bands of earth his feet.
They that stood and saw him die
Brushed the salt tear from the eye,
And they that wrapped him, by and by,
In his winding-sheet.

He was one that had high thought
In the mind-rooms where he wrought
For all others' sake;

And had looked along the way,
Where the halting-places lay,
Where, from every weary day,
He his rest would take.

December, 1846.

THE CHRIST FORGOTTEN IN OUR DAYS.

"Though He was rich, yet, for our sakes, He became poor. — How hardly shall they that have riches enter into the kingdom of God! — The cares of this life, and the deceitfulness of riches choke the Word, and it becometh unfruitful. — Lay not up for yourselves treasures upon earth. — Take no thought for the morrow."

CHRIST in a wretched place was born,
Nor owned his very grave;
He lived both homeless and forlorn, —
His fellows such as rich men scorn, —
And ate what beggars gave.

And when the Lord of Life became
Poor, and of none esteem,
He bade his followers do the same;
For Him to choose a life of shame;
Earth's goods a curse to deem.

The poor He blessed, and opened wide
The kingdom to their feet;
And bade the rich man go divide
The wealth whereon he built his pride,
And give the poor to eat.

Not otherwise might he be made
Christ's brother and God's son;
For how could one in pomp arrayed
The family of Christ invade,
Where wealth and pomp was none?

Christ's brethren, — oh! what seraphim
Cared less for earthly good!
The rich, bright world to them was dim;
They marched along with Prayer and Hymn,
And left it, where it stood.

If in the Kingdom's early day,
Men gave up earth for Heaven,
If lands and wealth they gave away,
If dainty food and rich array, —
If all for Christ was given,

Then how unlike God's humble Son
Are they who bear his name!
In rich apparel every one,
No worldly good they care to shun:
Are those and these the same?

The rich, — the rich are everywhere;
These fill the Temple too,

And scantly give the poor a share
To whom Christ said YE BLESSED ARE:
God's kingdom is for you.

O rich men! who do claim to be
The followers of the Lamb,
What, what are you, and what was He?
Is not His name a mockery?
Is not your faith a sham?

I see your houses cedar-lined:
Ye feed each earthborn lust
For food, for gems, for gold refined,
For every pleasure that can bind
The spirit down to dust.

What single thing that wealth can buy
Do ye, for Christ, forget?
TO BEAR THY CROSS, THYSELF DENY,—
Know ye these words? Were they to die,
Or are they living yet?

Has Christ taught you another way,
The Fathers never knew,
To live well here, and live for aye?
To have the riches earth can pay,
And those hereafter too?

And yet ye cant of serving God
And giving to his poor,
Who go unfed, unclothed, unshod,
And underneath the heavy sod
First find a sleep secure.

O men well clothed, and warmed, and filled
While God's poor children fast,
The very churches that ye build
And deck with pomp and carve and gild
Will judge you at the last.

WHERE ARE MY POOR, Christ still demands,—
To whom the Gospel came?
This costly offering at your hands
Is to yourselves, and only stands
A monument of shame.

GIVE TO MY POOR! give much: give all,
If nothing less will do;
They that at first obeyed the call,
Were fain to let earth's riches fall:
Shall I ask less of you?

June, 1849.

THE PITYING CHRIST.*

O MY Saviour! art Thou there?
From within this wasted heart,
Cries of shame and deep woe start:
Empty chambers, empty halls,
Everywhere some lone voice calls:
There dwelt pleasure; there came sin:
Wailing sounds now roam within.
Saviour! Oh! if Thou art there,
Be my heart of all else bare!

O my Saviour! art Thou there?
Otherwheres I looked, too long;
Till I read thy dear looks wrong;
Love on others I have thrown,
And my Lord have all unknown.
Now, by loss and sorrow wise,
Let me look up to thine eyes!
Lord! if Thou, indeed, be there,
Give thy prodigal his share!

* "Christ may dwell in your hearts by faith."

NEWFOUNDLAND.

O RUGGED land!
Land of the rock moss!
Land whose drear barrens it is woe to cross!
Thou rough thing from God's hand!
O stormy land!
Land where the tempests roar!
Land where the unbroken waves rave mad upon
the shore:
Thine outwalls scarce withstand!

O wintry realm,
Where the cold north winds blow;
Where drifting, bitter sleet, and blinding snow
All man's poor work o'erwhelm!
O bleak, bleak realm,
Whose homeward-hastening bark
Is crisped with ice: sails, cordage, stiff and stark,
And iced the unruly helm!

What hast thou in thy gift?
The kindly sun has shone,
These thousand years, the stubborn cliffs upon

Which thou on high dost lift:
What hast thou in thy gift?
A stinted growth appears:
Grass, shrub, and tree, slow-growing in long
years,
Where gapes the rocky rift.

Yet thou art good:
Thy barrens feed the deer;
And birds of other lands do summer here,
In thy lone humble wood.
Ay, thou art good;
The poor man at his door
Gathers his fuel; and year-long thy shore
Yields, in free gift, his food.

And better, still:
Beneath a guardian-crown
The poor man freely walks and lays him down,
Free in all things but ill:
And better, still:
Here Holy Faith hath come,
Teaching that God will give a glorious home
To those that do His will.

January 9, 1847.

TO THE MUSE—NEVER OLD.

Dear Muse! thou hast not told me wrong:
  Thou wert a heavenly thing:
I knew it in the earliest song
  I learned of thee to sing.

I took thee at thy simple word
  (And none like thee was fair);
Thy whisper's breath my life all stirred,
  And the chill touch of thy hair.

For thee I watched the twilight soft;
  For thee I roamed the wood;
Unwaited and unlooked for, oft,
  Beside me thou hast stood.

The sunlight I learned all with thee:
  The gleam and gloom of rill:
All lonely glories of the sea,
  And woods with full thought still;

Broad sheen of night-time, and its shade;
  The stars' great, awful walk;
Whatever sundered stillness made
  More dear than men's best talk:

And finer things than ear can take,
  More fair than eye can know,
From God's clear realm some slightest flake,
  That melts with us, below.

With thee I saw the flush of cheek,
  The truth of moist, deep eye:
Life's hidden tide, where no sunbeams leak,
  As whirl its strong depths by.

The craft of words is thy dear gift,
  That struggling hearts can hold,
And sudden, wondrous building lift
  In thought's broad sky of gold.

Come, yet, to me! chill days are here,
  When earth's fresh things are shed,
And hearts hold closer all their dear
  For want of all their dead.

October, 1863.

TO MY FRIEND LONG SUNDERED.

THUS we meet, that long were parted:
  As I feel thy hand,
Seems, once more, the boy, high-hearted,
  By my side to stand.

Now thy touch is something colder
  Than 'twas wont to be;
We are changed in growing older:
  Yet I longed for thee:

Waited anxiously, yet fearing
  For the change of years;
Hoped yet dreaded thy appearing
  To shape out my fears.

For our feelings grew together,
  And our voices, blent,

Through the long fair summer weather,
Forth in space were sent.

Every answering hill that heard them
Called them not apart;
They were one; one impulse stirred them,
Mingled from each heart.

By the solemn forest shaded,
Side by side we lay;
Hand in hand the streamlet waded,
Tossing far its spray.

Many a tree and hill and hollow
Fondly then we knew;
Many a lonely path could follow,
Where light glimmered through.

At the fence the wood dividing
Lay our common spoil,
Hidden for the sake of hiding,
Treasured for the toil.

Every frequent boyish pleasure,
Lost, if had alone,
We would share it without measure!
Thine was still my own.

Every sight of love and beauty
  That to childhood came;
Every hope and every duty;
  Dreams that had no name; —

Each with each to us was blended,
  And one shadow threw:
To one bourne the shadows tended,
  Over life's wide view.

When apart, an anxious longing
  In our hearts was set;
And our pulses, loud and thronging,
  Bounded as we met.

Hastily my veins would tingle
  At thy noble deed;
And thy glance of praise, though single,
  Was my dearest meed.

Now thy voice is calm and steady,
  And thine eye is cold;
And the glow that once was ready
  Comes not, as of old.
We that had one record, only,
  From the Angel's pen,

Now, long separate and lonely,
  Are no more as then.

Fare thee well! I could not greet thee
  After darker change.
Let it be enough to meet thee
  Now not wholly strange.

November, 1839.

THE CRY OF THE WRONGED.

The allusion, in the fourth stanza, to the startling emptiness of the hovel from which one of those poor people, who are just suffered to live in this world, has gone to another, will be recognized in full force by any one who has, even once in his life, looked in upon such a sight. I have seen, on untwisting the string from the nail and pushing open the crazy door, literally almost no relics but the handful of ashes upon the hearth, and the little heap of dust, laid out upon the bench, waiting to be given back to the earth from which it was taken. God help our poor brethren!

Brother, I am only dust:
Wherefore wilt thou be unjust?
Wherefore shake my humble trust
In our God, my brother?
There is yet but little day
That together we shall stay:
Wherefore jostle me away?
Love we one another.

I have but this little spot:
From my poor need snatch it not:
It is all that I have got
Of this hard world's giving.
Is there not a room for me,
Among all God made to be,
Where to gather, manfully,
Yet with toil my living?

God has given light and air:
Grudge not thou my little share;
Lo! it cometh everywhere,
We may share together.
God, Himself, has set me here,
And, with many a bitter tear,
I have struggled many a year
Of rough and wintry weather.

Let me work, — I ask no more,—
Till my stint is labored o'er.
I can never lay up store;
None this world will send me.
When I go, if men look there,
They will find my place all bare;
Nothing but the light and air,
God was good to lend me.

Brother, look at me again:
Toil has given me many a stain,
Toil has swollen every vein,
Yet I am thy brother.
I am man, as well as thou,
And our Lord has crossed my brow,
Calling me God's child, and how
Wilt thou call me other?

Let me stay until He call:
Let me stay till evening fall,
If so long I must be thrall,
Earth's hard labor plying.
When thou comest to take share
In my cold bed, thou wilt there
Grant my claim, and little care
Near the poor man lying.

December, 1846.

A CHRISTMAS SERMON.

On the glorious Birthday morning,
All the church is dressed in green;
Loud are heard the holy anthems,
Sweetest prayers go up between.

He that lay in lowly manger,
Now is known as Heaven's King;
What but angels sang, aforetime,
Now have men been taught to sing:

"God have glory, in the highest:
Peace on earth, good-will towards men:
Over all the tide of ages,
Ever now as it was then."

After prayers and chant all ended,
Then the priest begins to preach:
In God's name he speaketh plainly,
For God's sake he loveth each.

"Lo!" he saith, "the Lord of Glory,
Born and cradled in a stall!
Sure He had but scanty welcome,
Seeing He was Lord of all.

"Yet, in sooth, He sought no other,
Nor to earth for homage came;
Here He took the form of servant;
Here He bared the cheek to shame.

"Not of this world was His kingdom:
He lived not at monarch's cost:
He sought not the known and honored,
But He came to seek the lost:

"Lost from out the world's long annals,
For they came of humble kin:
Lost from out the Book of Heaven,
For their life was led in sin.

"Thus the poor, and thus the sinner,
Found the Lord beside their door:
Heard His blessed words of comfort,
Such as no man spake before.

"Let our thoughts, this day, my brethren,
Seek the poor, by men forgot;

Whom the holy Christ remembered,
Coming here to share their lot.

"This world hath its rich and needy:
This world hath its high and low:
On the one side, pomp and worship;
On the other, toil and woe.

"Not forever shall we struggle
With the trials of this state:
To be poor, and yet be thankful;
To be lowly-willed, if great.

"Yet a little, and the Judgment:
Then we change for good or ill:
Rich or poor shall enter heaven,
As they did the Father's will.

"To be rich we may not covet,
Ye have heard the Saviour say:
And He chose the lowest station
When He came to earth this day.

"He has told us of His kingdom,
Hardly shall the rich go in;
Though the best that this world offers, —
Power and glory, — wealth may win.

"I will tell a simple story:
Every day it falleth true;
Jesu grant you all, my brethren,
That it be not so of you.

"See you there how Dives sitteth,
Richly clad, at dainty fare?
Many servants make obeisance,
Many guests sit humbly there.

"Now one cometh, speaking softly,
'Lazarus is at the gate:
Waiting, in full mournful fashion,
That his welcome cometh late.

"'For he meekly claimeth kindred,
Though he is of low degree.'
Heed the rich man, now, my brethren:
Scornful answer maketh he:

"'Lazarus? I know no beggars,
And my kin bear no such name:
Yet these poor folk have their kindred;
Bid him go from whence he came.'

"'Good my lord, the dogs are licking,
In mere ruth, his running sore;

He is modest, and he claimeth
But the crumbs from off thy floor.'

"'Prating varlet!' said the rich man,
'Now what idle knaves have I!
Was there none to bid this beggar
Choose a fitter place to die?'

"He forgot that in God's heaven,
Righteous poor shall have their share:
And he thrust him from the threshold,
Caring nought how he might fare.

"So the servants laid the beggar
Just before another's gate;
Coming back, with due obeisance,
At their master's side to wait.

"Soon the poor man died, full godly,
And with saints he went to dwell:
Next the rich man died, and, after,
Lifted up his eyes in hell;

"And afar he saw the poor man,
As he lay in Abraham's breast;
And, from out his place of torment,
Prayed towards that blissful rest.

"'T was but for a drop of water:
Yet his boon he could not win:
God had set a gulf, forever,
'Twixt the two that were not kin.

"For the words of dreadful judgment,
Christ hath told us what they be:
'I was hungry, sick, and naked,
And ye had no care of me.'

"Then shall they make forward answer,
That on earth had Him forgot:
'Lord, when saw we Thee an-hungered,
Sick, and naked, and cared not?'

"Christ shall say, 'These poor and wretched,
Whose meek claim ye put aside,
I do own them as my brethren,
And in them was I denied.

"'When ye saw me not, nor heard me,
It was I put up the claim:
I lay pining at the threshold,
For they sought you in my name.'

"Let us, then, confess Christ's brother,
Lest we claim another kin:

Then, before the gate of heaven,
He shall bid us enter in.

" Glory, worship, love, and service,
To the blessed One in Three:
As it was in the beginning,
Is, and evermore shall be!"

BEFORE MORNS.*

STAY not at the open door:
Hear the soft pipes calling sweetly;
Bow thy head to enter meetly;
It is just the Prayers before.
Now, in secret prayer to heaven,
Set thy knees upon the floor:
Humbly wait till God has given
That He gives forevermore;
Welcome to bright youth and maiden,
To the worn and very heavy laden,
To the wounded and the sore.
To His children He comes hither;
His fair glory fills this place;
Earth-born things, earth's day will wither;
But fresh life grows in God's gifts of grace.

He will bless thee: ask Him lowly;
Let thine heart be open wide:

* May we not commonly say "Morns" and "Eves" in our own tongue, for our Church-services?

But bethink thee, naught unholy, —
Lust, — dark hatred, — base sloth, —
pride, —
May thy heart hold fast, or slowly,
Sadly, He will turn aside;
Thou wilt be unjustified.

Has thy heart before Him bended?
Keep not to thyself, alone;
Let thy voice with these be blended:
For the world these make their moan
That God's grace may far be thrown:
And till this great hour is ended,
Count all others as thine own.

THE PALMER AT THE WAYSIDE, RESTING.

WHAT we once lost, may we ever have back;
That brightest, that one brightest thing, of our all;
Whose want has so often made sunshine look black,
And turned our writhed faces, in tears, to the wall?

Maiden's fair name? Or the young cheek's pure shame?
Or man's trusty faith, or his quick will to dare?
Or love, that to woman and man is the same;
What, lost, chills earth's warmth, and takes life from its air?

No! — We may never more see what we lost,
Though standing, with backward look, all the short day.
Another may wear it, or haply have tost,
Unknowing its worth, what we mourn for, away.

Nay, — what we lost, that can never be, more ;
But broken, or trampled, or sullied, or torn,
No likeness will be of the look it once wore,
Save that in our poor hearts so faithfully borne.

Maiden, untaught, yet, that torn hearts will cling,
And man, proudly choosing to doubt that which
seems,
Oh, never, to you, may the one brightest thing
Be that which then only in memory gleams !

Bitter to think, and most bitter to yearn !
Ah ! bitter to know that our hand was too slack !
With naught, then, but praying for meek hearts,
to learn
That dear things, once lost, we shall never have
back !

If, then, in tenderness God after give
Some new priceless thing, with more wise heed
to wear,
(For hearts must still love, or be dead while
they live,)
Then leave to the past what was lightly lost
there.

August 7, 1862.

THE BISHOP BOUND.

[After a missionary bishop had been sent out to Jerusalem, by the English Church, a great storm was raised in England, because he suffered some members of the superstitious and decrepid Eastern Church, in the midst of which he stood, to learn the Gospel of him.]

"Necessity is laid upon me."

YE tell me that I must not preach
The Gospel to these men,
And if it struggles up to speech,
Must choke it down — and then? —

I may stand here, with dimming eyes,
And watch the world abroad;
For what? — Lest they, in any wise,
Should catch the truth of God.

They have "Most Holy Lords" to reign
Where poor Apostles wrought:
Shall "Right Divine" God's work restrain
And bring His Faith to nought?

Can tapers, robes, and painted saints,
And chant of old-time words
Save, more than flowers that sunlight paints,
Or out-door song of birds?

If living faith in God's own Son
Alone true life can give,
Shall I undo what God has done,
Nor bid these dead men live?

The winds are His, as well as I,
And, as their quick feet flit,
They will not let the message die
But men shall hear of it.

Could ye stand by me in my need,
When the last Judge is set,
And all is done, of human deed,
But not accounted, yet?

Oh, no! this breath I breathe, of air,
And shape in words, to-day,
Must preach His Gospel everywhere,
Or woe is mine for aye.

January 15, 1854.

THE PRIEST THAT MUST BE.

THOU art to be a priest in holy things;
A minister of thy great Maker, God!
Oh! all of earth that to thy earth-heart clings, —
And all the bribe-gifts that the fair world brings, —
All that the Tempter's voice most sweetly sings,
Calling thy spirit to come forth, abroad,
Oh, not for thee, — they must not be for thee!
What they have been, no more must ever be.

In Christ's eternal priesthood thou wilt share,
To reconcile to God His sinful sons:
Ambassador for God, thou, too, shalt wear
His very person, and thy tongue shall dare
In Christ's stead, to beseech the erring ones.
Who is enough for this far-reaching work?
At whose poor heart doth not the vile worm lurk?
This priceless trust in earthen case is set:
Who holds it falls, if he do once forget
In God's gift, only, might and worth are met.

When, in Christ's name and stead, thou shalt
beseech,
His loving Gospel to the others preach,
And pledges of God's grace share forth to
each ; —
When other hearts lie open to thine own,
Eyes trusting look to thee, as on a throne ; —
Nothing but Christ's rich blood can for thyself
atone.

Bethink thee, well, how one may speak true
blame
Of deadly sin and load it thick with shame ;
One may bear charge for God and take Christ's
name,
And yet, at Reckoning, may be cast off,
A woe to loving ones, to fiends a scoff.
But oh, what deeper loss shall his be, then,
Who, of his priesthood, made a lure to men !
Who drew in weaker souls, and led them wrong :
His Gospel but a witching, wicked song !
Where, out of God's great love, shall that bad
wretch belong !

Lift up thy faith beyond the inner sky
Where, in deep peace, God ever sits on high :

Amid all sounds which meet there in His
praise, —
Which worlds and hosts, cherubs and seraphs
raise
To Him, far off and near, Ancient of Days,
One, only God, thrice holy Three in One,
Beyond time's death, as ere time was begun,
There He that calls thee in dread stillness sits,
While, flashing everywhere, high, glorious music
flits.

To Him the rain-drop, plashing on the sea,
The winged seed wafted from the forest-tree,
The insect's gaspings, and the sun's swift ray
Kindling up countless atoms in its way,
Each after each, to bring to earth the day,
All, all are heard, — all things are heard, —
yet He
Hears thy thoughts moving in the midst of thee.
Let not the busy world, with its loud din,
Let not the sweet, enticing calls of sin,
Let nothing draw thine ear from God's still voice
within!

He sees thee all; the flashing of an eye;
The changing cheek; the bosom swelling high;

Yea, the first impulse of the peaceful blood,
Ere, with fell passion's surge, it rushes to its flood.
He sees the little pictures spread within
Thy mind's deep chambers, where no eye ca win:
As if no other thing on earth's smooth face,
But thou, alone, in clearest light had place,
As if He looked on thee and thee alone,
Thus open standest thou: thus seen, thus known.
Look not on wrong, nor let the Tempter dare
To find a back-way up into thy heart,
And open all his cursed, tempting ware
To bargain with thee for thy better part.
Thou hast no secrets that are hid from God;
Thine inmost places by His feet are trod:
Hast thou sin, there? it lies before His sight:
Die, if thou must, but cast it from thee, quite!

If thou hast ever taken gifts of Hell
And then repented, and hast thrown them out,
And swept all clean (while bloody tear-drops fell)
And scattered holy balms, the place about;
Search yet again; thou knowest but too well

If thine own hand have somewhere laid away
Some sin that penitence might overlook,
To come to light, some time, and draw astray
Thy weaker thoughts, or, at the Dreadful Day,
To stand revealed, and damn thee from God's
Book.

The Spirit, — like the wind that wears no form
In wooing summer-breath, or ruthless storm, —
Breaks up the dark heart's strongly-frozen deep,
Or lays the whirl of earthly lusts to sleep.
He, only, is thy strength and warmth and light:
Trust well thy faith in Him, where faith is
sight.

Half, Sept., 1846: half, July 29, 1863.

A COMMUNING WITH GOD

BEFORE ENTERING INTO HOLY ORDERS.

WHAT hands will now be laid upon me, Lord?
Whose spirit breathed, whose blessed influence
given?
By whom shall I be sent to bear The Word —
That precious load — along the path to Heaven?

Almighty God! Eternal God! 'T is Thou,
That in Thy chosen servant here dost stand:
Prostrate before Thy footstool, lo, I bow,
To seek the dread commission at Thy hand.

O God, the Father! from whose quickening
breath
All beings move, each in his proper round,
Whosè arm sustains, above the abyss of Death,
What èlse would sink within that dread pro-
found,

Give me, Great Parent, that enkindling power
To wake anew, deep in my brother's soul,
The Godlike nature, that, in man's first hour,
Made the dim part reflect the perfect whole.

O God, the Son! who, with unbounded grace,
Tookést up manhood, healedst the gaping wound,
And barést to the Father's dwelling-place
The dying saved, the long-lost wanderer found,

Give unto me that ready neighbor-love,
That guideth where the wounded heart to find;
And give me Thy blest unction from above,
With holy balm the bleeding soul to bind.

O God, the Holy Ghost! that hallowest all
Thy faithful people, and to every truth
Upwards their still advancing steps dost call,
Till weary Age rests, smiling back on youth,

Hallow my life, that I may ever be
Worthy to stand at my King's festal board;
And teach me truth, that, being taught by
Thee,
I may show others where all good is stored.

One only God! whose works and ways are one,
Grant me with single heart to do Thy will,
Make me wrong thoughts and words and ways
to shun,
In Thy one, mystic realm my place to fill.

Keith Hall, Bermudas,
November 29, 1842, at night.

THE RELIEF OF LUCKNOW.

Are there not many that remember (who can forget?) that scene in the Sikh war, — also in India, — when the distant gleam of arms and flash of friendly uniform was descried by a little exhausted army among the hills, and the Scotch pipes struck up "*Oh! but ye were lang a-comin!*" (Lachrymamne teneatis, amici? None of us, that have much Scottish blood, can keep our eyes from moistening.) The incident in the present case *may* not be historical, but it is true to nature, and intrinsically probable, which is all that poetry needs, in that respect.

Oh! that last day in Lucknow fort!
We knew that it was the last;
That the enemy's mines had crept surely in,
And the end was coming fast.

To yield to that foe meant worse than death;
And the men and we all worked on:
It was one day more, of smoke and roar,
And then it would all be done.

There was one of us, a Corporal's wife,
A fair, young, gentle thing,

Wasted with fever in the siege,
And her mind was wandering.

She lay on the ground, in her Scottish plaid,
And I took her head on my knee;
"When my father comes hame frae the pleugh," she said,
"Oh! please then waken me."

She slept like a child on her father's floor,
In the flecking of woodbine-shade,
When the house-dog sprawls by the half-open door,
And the mother's wheel is stayed.

It was smoke and roar and powder-stench,
And hopeless waiting for death;
But the soldier's wife, like a full-tired child,
Seemed scarce to draw her breath.

I sank to sleep, and I had my dream
Of an English village-lane,
And wall and garden; — a sudden scream
Brought me back to the roar again.

There Jessie Brown stood listening,
And then a broad gladness broke

All over her face, and she took my hand
And drew me near and spoke:

"*The Highlanders!* Oh! dinna ye hear?
The slogan far awa?
The McGregor's? Ah! I ken it weel;
It's the grandest o' them a'.

"God bless thae bonny Highlanders!
We're saved! We're saved!" she cried;
And fell on her knees, and thanks to God
Poured forth, like a full flood-tide.

Along the battery-line her cry
Had fallen among the men:
And they started; for they were there to die;
Was life so near them, then?

They listened, for life; and the rattling fire
Far off, and the far-off roar
Were all; — and the Colonel shook his head,
And they turned to their guns once more.

Then Jessie said, "That slogan's dune;
But can ye no hear them, noo,
'*The Campbells are comin'*? It's no a dream;
Our succors hae broken through!"

We heard the roar and the rattle afar,
But the pipes we could not hear;
So the men plied their work of hopeless war,
And knew that the end was near.

It was not long ere it must be heard;
A shrilling, ceaseless sound;
It was no noise of the strife afar,
Or the sappers underground.

It *was* the pipes of the Highlanders,
And now they played '*Auld Lang Syne:*"
It came to our men, like the voice of God,
And they shouted along the line.

And they wept and shook one another's hands,
And the women sobbed in a crowd;
And every one knelt down where we stood,
And we all thanked God aloud.

That happy day, when we welcomed them,
Our men put Jessie first;
And the General took her hand, and cheers
From the men, like a volley, burst.

And the pipers' ribbons and tartan streamed,
Marching round and round our line;

And our joyful cheers were broken with tears,
For the pipes played "*Auld Lang Syne.*"

Saturday and Sunday nights,
January 2 and 3, 1858.

THE PAST THAT IS NOT OURS.

Let us forget the Past!
It may have been both bright and dear:
Another world is here;
It was not made to last;
Let us forget: 't is past!

Take, if you will, once more,
The fading memories in hand:
In old thought once more stand;
Then fling them from the shore!
Ours they can be no more.

Youth, to our far-off eyes,
Seems glad with beams of better light:
It only cheats the sight:
There were spring's changeful skies:
Let us not turn our eyes!

Here is our own fair time:
Here God has spread His blessed day;

The fresh breeze comes this way;
This is a better clime:
Why shall we mourn that time?

We shall go farther, yet:
And bear our wayside harvest dried:
Our friends shall go beside;
The Past we may forget:
Our way leads forward, yet.

July 30. 1863.

DIRGE TO A SOUL DEPARTING.

(FOR MUSIC.)

STAY, flitting soul!
Wilt thou not longer stay?
Why dost thou hasten on that weary way,
Beyond these quiet realms of day,
Into the unknown land, where dim mists roll?
Look back! Look back
Along the well-known track,
Stretching far backward to dear scenes of spring!
There childhood's pretty memories lie:
The flowing hair, the beamy eye,
The bounding step, and joyous, ringing cry.
See the glad hopes that erst
The child's true spirit nurst,
By day in visions bright,
In whispering dreams by night;
Dost thou not yearn towards them, as we sing?
And youth's first real strife

With the breasting waves of life,
When strength was in the arm,
And the heart was proud and warm,
And the eye looked forth, without alarm,
For all that time could bring.
See, see those sunny days!
And let our soft dirge raise
Bright tempting scenes before thine eye to fling!
Look! Look! This world is bright;
But now thou loved'st its light;
Why dost thou turn away thy sight,
As from an evil thing?
Come to us back! Come to us back!
Let not our sorrowing spirits lack
The fellowship to which our strong loves cling!

[*Weeping stillness.*]

Is it so hard for thee to linger yet
Where thou hast been at home these many
years?
Why should these long-familiar lendings fret
Now, more than ever, that thou fain wilt set
This pleasant form aside, that we with tears
Must wash; then put away
Out of our sight forever and for aye?

Come to us back! Come to us back!
Come, yet a little, to our fond hearts back!

[*Stillness.*]

Why, why would'st thou forget
These once-loved voices, that, in every tone,
In days gone by, sweet influence have thrown
Around thee, answering warmly to thine own?
Wilt thou not listen? Hast thou no regret?
Wilt thou still forward, where is all unknown?
Wilt thou still forward?
And alone?
Oh, wilt thou venture such a path alone?
Turn! Turn! Come back! Come back!
Before thee how it gathers black!
Return, where all thou holdest dear are met!

[*Stillness.*]

Thou loiterest still;
We see these casements fill
With the soft-falling, gentle mist
Where thou art looking out, once more,
To see the scene long-known and loved before.

Hist! Hist!
This sternly-closéd door
From which glad words were wont to pour,
Is it forever closed? Will it not open more?
Is it in vain we list?
We mark, we mark its fixéd leaves
Tremble, as the soul still heaves
Against them feebly, as in doubt
To open yet to us that wait without;
Come, then! Oh, come!

[*Stillness.*]

But that faint, smothered cry!
Ah, smothered strife of agony!
Nay! we will let this weary body die!
Nay! flitting spirit, nay!
We will not have thee stay;
Go forward gladly on thy way;
Our songs shall cheer thee as thou goest home.

Farewell! Farewell! Close we these open eyes.
No more wilt thou be looking forth, this way,
Who once hast caught, afar, the light of Paradise.

Our love shall give this form to long decay,
That, when thou comest back for it, shall rise
A glorious body, at the Judgment-Day.

On! On! thou blessed soul! See Jesus wait;
Thy lamp of faith is trimmed, but all is light;
The path leads forward, to the open gate;
He waits thee smiling, and the way is bright.
On, faithful soul!
Our swelling songs shall roll
Sweet, melancholy surges here behind,
That full of memory thou shalt find,
As one, slow-sailing from the outward shore
Of a dear land oft wandered o'er,
Hears, in still night, its wave-voice on the
wind.
Thou art quitting, now, the verge
Of this long-belovéd land,
And mayest listen, still, the surge
Heave up upon the strand.
On! On! yet let our song
Still go with thee along,
'Till it is lost amid the strain
Of Christ's glorious spirit-train
As another soul they gain

To sweet Paradise, no more to live, no more to
love, as here on earth, in vain.
Our earth-born dirges cease:
Pass, Christian soul, in peace!
Peace that Christ giveth:
PEACE!

January, 1846.

THE MAIDEN OUTSIDE THE WORLD.

"Oh, this long, dull life at sea:
Day lagging into lagging night!"
The maiden sang, in the failing light:
"Forever sailing this sullen sea!
O Father, make sail, and leave me at land!
I see it broad on the larboard hand:
O Father, this life is death to me;
Forever holding the drowsy line,
Or drawing it drowsily in from the deep!
Thou art old: but youth, bright you this mine
Oh! why must I lean here, ever, and weep?
Make sail for land! It is nigh at hand:
Make sail for land! Make sail for land!
Once let me in God's fair garden stand,
And my slow blood shall leap.

"I see no land, but a fog-cloud low:
Long hours have we eyed it, looming so:

No current sets here: land is not near:
Be, Child, as thou wert, this short while ago:
Think not of the land that thou dost not know!"

Thus many a young heart, on Life's sea,
Will long for the far land under the lee;
And many a heart that time has tried
Will strive from the far land to keep it wide.

THE YEAR IS GONE!

WHERE art thou, O lost Year?
I tread upon the scattered leaves,
The way is drear, my lone heart grieves.
I see thy traces everywhere;
These leaves once decked thy golden hair:
I find thy playthings here;
But oh! thou art not near.

The bright and golden grain —
Men have it all long garnered in.
Here spreads the frosted stubble, thin,
O'er the wide fields whereon it stood,
Where thou didst trip, in playful mood,
Bringing the sun or rain.
I seek for thee in vain.

Is this thy merry brook,
Whose gurgling used to please thine ear?
Oh! my once happy, thoughtless Year!

Beneath its solid, icy roof,
How silent, now, it bides aloof!
Lost is the frolic look
That from thy smile it took.

Beneath the forest tall
No more I feel thy glowing breath,
Or watch the calm, too bright for death,
When thou at noon didst fall asleep,
And, what thy hands could no more keep,
Blossom or nut, would fall,
Sweet Year! In vain I call.

Thy pretty birds are mute,
That sang with all their little might
And flashed their bright wings in the light:
And children, fairer still than they,
Gambol no longer at their play:
No more the busy foot
Tramples the soft grass-root.

Thou wert no more the same
When once that hectic flush of red
Too surely on thy fair cheek spread;
And, by and by, in silent fold,
The white robes closed, all still and cold,

And when I called thy name,
No voice or answer came.

And there was deeper bond
Than such as various season weaves,
Of sunny flowers, or buds, or leaves:
I mourn for many a hope and thought
That by thy ministry were brought
Out of the world beyond:
These made my poor heart fond.

And I have wrought with thee,
In pleasant hours, at many a net,
Of hues, as when the sun doth set.
We stretched the strands out very wide,
But each too soon was thrust aside:
New schemes thou broughtest me
Of what could never be.

Thou knewest all I willed;
How many purposes I made:
Into thine ear the whole was said,
How I would rue the ill deeds done,
How guilty temptings I would shun.
Now thy warm life is chilled,
What, of these plans, fulfilled!

O lost Year, be thou past!
Too soon the truant heart and will
All this clear sky of life would fill
With that unprofitable haze,
That makes half nights of working days.
Forward my way is cast;
I rest not till the last.

1849.

A ROBIN'S SONG, AFTER LONG WINTER.

WHAT ear and eye, in the spring's first days,
Is not drawn to that happy songster's lays?
Quick, — glad, — strong, —
And then so wondrous-wondrous-feat,
More wondrous as more long,
It seemed from under some brooding heat
Gladness and song and skill had sprung
In a flash of spring-life, fresh and young;
Then died as suddenly, the glad skilled song
once sung.

BÜRGER'S LENORE.

LENORA rose at morning-red,
From bitter dreams awaking:
"Art faithless, William, or art dead,
So long thy love forsaking?"
He went with royal Frederic's might,
To battle in Prague's famous fight:
But from the war-field gory
No post has brought his story.

The King and Empress, tired, at last,
Of arms so vainly wielded,
Alike aside their rage have cast,
And to a truce have yielded.
Now each glad host with sing-song rang,
With beating drum and cling and clang;
And, decked with many a garland,
Came homeward from the far land.

And over all, all over all,
From street and lane and alley,

Shout old and young their jubel-call,
And round the home-march rally.
Praise God! the child and goodwife cried;
Welcome! said many a longing bride;
But, for Lenore, no meeting:
No kiss, or tender greeting.

Each way she flew, the ranks all through,
But, though all names were spoken,
No one that came her lover knew,
And no one could give token.
And when the hosts passed onward were,
She tore her glossy, raven hair;
Upon the greensward sinking,
With bitter woe past thinking.

The mother kneeled upon her knee;
"God, pity my poor daughter!
My darling child, what is't with thee?"
And in her arms she caught her.
"Ah, mother, mother, gone is gone!
Now let the world and all be gone! *
No pity dwells in Heaven:
Woe! woe! my heart is riven!"

* Wherever a final word is repeated, the original has the same construction.

"Help, God! oh, help! look gently on!
Child, child! oh, say, 'Our Father!'
What God does, that is sure well done:
God, judge not; spare us rather!"
"O mother, mother, mockery!
God has not, sure, well-done to me.
My prayers, ah! what passed they for?
Now nought is left to pray for!"

"Help, God! whoe'er the Father knows,
Knows He the children loveth;
The Holy Sacrament such woes
As thine, my child, removeth."
"O mother, mother, little vent
My woe would find in sacrament.
No sacrament can solder
Forms that in death-damps moulder."

"Hear, child! How if the perjured one,
When long in far Hungáry,
Had all his ties of troth undone,
Some newer love to marry?
Fling off his heart, my child! by sin
In the long game he cannot win;
When soul and body sever,
This deed shall sting forever"

"O mother, mother, gone is gone!
Forsaken is forsaken;
Death, death! Come death, and I have won!
Why did I ever waken?
Go out, forever out, my light!
Die out, die out, in woe and night!
No pity dwells in Heaven;
Woe! woe! my soul is riven!"

"Help, God! To judgment enter not:
The poor child's heart is broken:
She utters, now, she knows not what:
Oh, count not what is spoken!
My child, forget this world's distress,
And think on God, and blessedness:
So to thy heart forsaken
A spouse shall yet be taken."

"O mother! What is blessedness?
Oh! what is hell, my mother?
With him, with him, is blessedness;
And hell without him, mother.
Go out, forever out, my light!
Die out, die out, in woe and night!
Without him, earth and heaven
In misery were even."

Thus mad despair within her brain,
And in her veins all revelled,
Till e'en at God's all-gracious reign,
Her impious scorn she levelled.
She wrung her hands and beat her breast
Until the sun went down to rest:
Till up to heaven's high chamber
The golden stars 'gan clamber.

And then without, hark! tramp, tramp, tramp!
A horse's footsteps sounded;
Then on the steps, with heavy stamp,
The clanking rider bounded.
And hark! and hark! the door-bell ring,
All gently, softly, cling-ling-ling.
Then, through the door-leaves uttered,
Just these quick questions fluttered:

"Holla! holla! undo, my child!
Wak'st thou, my love, or sleepest?
Has time thy love for me beguiled?
And smilest thou, or weepest?"
"Ah, William! Thou, so late at night?
I've wept and waked, in weary plight;
Oh! bitter woe I've tasted.
Whence hast thou hither hasted?"

"Near midnight 't is, we saddle steed;
From Boehmen I rode hither:
Ere I could mount, 't was late indeed,
And we go back together."
"O William, first a moment stay:
The blast roars through the hawthorn spray,
Come to my arms, heart-dearest!
Here no cold wind thou fearest."

"Through hawthorn spray let fierce blasts roar,
And ravage, helter-skelter!
The wild steed paws, and clinks the spur;
I dare not here seek shelter.
Come, dress thee: spring and swing, with
speed,
Behind me, here, upon my steed.
A hundred miles I take thee,
This day my bride to make thee."

"Alas! a hundred miles would'st thou
Bear me, *this day*, to bridal?
Hark, hark! the clock is clanging now;
Eleven struck: 'T is idle!"
"Look far; look near; the moon shines
clear;
We and the dead ride fast, my dear;

I gage, ere night's at highest,
Thou in thy bride-bed liest."

"Say on, where is thy chamber, dear?
What bride-bed dost thou tender?"
"Still, cool and small; far, far from here;
Six wide boards and two slender."
"Hast room for me?" "For thee and me:
Come, dress thee: mount; I stay for thee.
The marriage-guests have waited:
We must not be belated."

Fairly she dressed her, sprang and swung
Herself to horse behind him;
Fast to the well-loved rider clung,
And with white arms entwined him.
Then hurtling off, with leap and bound,
At whistling speed they scoured the ground,
Till horse and rider panted,
And sparks and dust far slanted.

On this and on the other hand,
How flew the plains and ridges;
Hillock and rock and meadow-land;
How thundered all the bridges!
"My love, dost fear? The moon shines clear:

Hurrah! The dead ride fast, my dear!
My love, dost fear the dead men?"
"Ah, no! yet leave the dead men!"

What clang and song swept there along,
Where the foul ravens flaunted?
Hark! death-bell clang! Hark! funeral-song!
"Bear on the dead!" is chanted.
And nearer drew a funeral-train:
Coffin and bier came on, amain:
Their song the dark quire pitches
Like the frogs' cry in ditches.

"Nay, bury after midnight-tide,
With clang and song and weeping:
I bear me home my fair young bride:
Come to our merry-keeping.
Come clerk! come here! your quire all bring,
Come all, the bridal-song to sing,
Come, priest, the blessing say us
Ere we in bride-bed lay us."

Ceased clang and song; the bier was gone:
They came as they were bidden,
And, hurry-skurry, trampled on
Fast as the steed was ridden.

And ever on, with leap and bound,
At whistling speed they scoured the ground;
Both horse and rider panted,
And sparks and dust far slanted.

How flew, on right, how flew, on left,
Hills, trees, and hedgéd spaces!
How flew, on left and right and left,
Towns, cities, dwelling-places!
"My love, dost fear? The moon shines clear:
Hurrah! The dead ride well, my dear;
My love, dost fear the dead men?"
"Ah! let them rest, the dead men!"

See there! see there! On gallows-height,
Dance round the wheel's curst swivel,
Half-seen within the moon's pale light,
Spectres, in airy revel.
"Sasa! ye spectres. Here! come here!
Come, spectres, come, and follow near,
Our wedding reels to number
Ere we lie down to slumber."

And lo! the spectres, rush, rush, rush!
Behind the wild train hurtle,

As whirls the storm-wind's sudden gush
Through withered leaves of myrtle.
And on and on, with leap and bound,
At whistling speed they scoured the ground;
Both horse and rider panted,
And sparks and dust far slanted.

How flew the scenes in moonlight spread!
How into farness flitted!
And how, their places overhead,
The sky and planets quitted!
"My love, dost fear? The moon shines
clear;
Hurrah! The dead ride well, my dear;
My love, dost fear the dead men?"
"Ah, woe! Let rest the dead men!"

"Steed, steed! methinks the cock crows
there;
Soon will the sands be wasted;
Steed, steed! I scent the morning air;
Haste, as thou hast not hasted!
'T is o'er, 't is o'er! Our course is o'er!
The chamber stands with open door;
The dead ride wondrous races:
Here, here, we find our places."

Against an iron churchyard door,
The furious courser battered:
Its clamps fell loose, the shock before,
And post and bar were shattered.
Its clanking leaves wide open flew,
And o'er the graves the train swept through.
Gravestones were seen to glimmer
Round in the moon's pale shimmer.

See, see! An instant scarce can flit,
Ere, hoo! a fearful wonder!
The rider's flesh, all bit by bit,
Like cinders fell asunder.
Like kernel bare, without the hull,
His head became a naked skull;
His body shrunk and narrow,
With hour-glass and with arrow.

Snorted the steed, and madly reared;
Fierce fiery flashes spurted;
Then hey! sank down and disappeared,
And she lay there deserted.
A howl, a howl from out the lift!
A yell from forth each grave's deep rift!
Lenora's spirit shivers:
'Twixt death and life it quivers.

Now featly danced, in moonlight-glance,
All round about in mazes,
The spectre-forms a fetter-dance,
And howled in such-like phrases;
"Be meek, though heart should break in
twain,
Nor dare thy God in heaven arraign.
Thy dust to this still city!
God show thy soul his pity!"

June, 1846.

THE BARREN FIELD.

Here I labor, weak and lone,
Ever, ever sowing seed;
Ever tending what is sown:
Little is my gain, indeed.

Weary day and restless night
Follow in an endless round;
Wastes my little human might:
Soon my place will not be found.

Why so stubborn is my field?
Why does little fruit appear?
What an hundred-fold should yield,
Now goes barren all the year.

Rank weeds crowd and jostle there,
Nodding vainly in the sun:
But the plants, for which I care,
I may tell them, one by one.

After all the sun and rain,
Weak and yellow drooping things,
From the lean earth, turned in vain,
These are all my labor wrings!

Oh, my Lord, the field is Thine:
Why do I, with empty pride,
Call the little garden mine,
When my work is Thine, beside?

If I claim it for my own,
Thou wilt give me its poor gain;
And, at harvest, I, alone,
May bring fruits to Thee in vain.

If I give myself to Thee
For Thy work, all poor and mean,
As Thou pleasest it shall be,
If I much or little glean:

Yet Thou wilt not spurn my toil,
Or my offering, at the last,
If, from off this meagre soil,
At Thy feet my all is cast.

Other work for man is none,
But to do the Master's will;
Wet with rain, or parched with sun,
Meekly I Thy garden till.

April 28, 1849.

CHRIST'S LEGACY.

Who deems that Holy Church has lost
  The priceless gift the Saviour gave?
Or, as an idle bauble, tost
  Beneath the curst world's hungry wave,
Her keys that, all this wide world o'er,
Oped to man's want God's spirit-store?
That now the Kingdom is but earth alone
Where man's poor sight and wisdom seek their
    own?

Who deems that hidden Paradise, —
  Its sweet cool shades, its living streams,
Its lustrous air, from seraph's eyes
  Radiant with interwoven beams,
And the eternal Light divine
Filling up all with changeless shine, —
That these, and converse with the dwellers there,
To men in spirit are not free as air?

That His blest kingdom, — which, Christ said,
  Should ever stand while earth doth stand,
And, when the last flames, fierce and red,
  Should melt and burn up sea and land,
Transfigured through those fires should glow
Thenceforth no earthliness to know, —
That this hath not one, only, changeless frame,
One as the Lord: on earth, in heaven, the same?

Or that the Body of the Lord,
  The Godhead dwelling in the flesh, —
Is not, to us, as when that Word
  In human nature dwelt afresh?
Or that God's fulness, now, as then,
Doth not inhabit in us men,
A fulness that in each of us hath place
Of grace according to our growth in grace?

Oh! is not God the selfsame now
  As when he put on human frame?
His Body is the Church: and how
  Is this, his Body, not the same?
It is the same where'er Faith is:
Christ manifests himself in His:
Where Faith is not, to them is Christ no more
Indwelling, in the Spirit, as of yore.

This glorious kingdom — rich within,
  And glowing with all spirit-powers —
There is no cause, but each man's sin,
  If all its treasures be not ours:
Our priests are gifted with the Word,
And every member of the Lord
Hath his own measure of the Holy Ghost:
In the most humble and obedient, most.

And in the Spirit, oh, what height
  The feet of faithful men do mount!
There glossy slopes flow all with light,
  And vales are rich with stream and fount.
The pure see God on every side;
Them spirits gently serve and guide;
While earth, to them, is sorrow, shame, and ill,
The church is heaven on earth, about them still.

Sweet mysteries to them that love,
  Do lead to that eye hath not seen;
An open sky is spread above
  Wherein no cloud hath ever been.
The Word wells full in every heart;
Deep calleth unto deep, apart;
And Love, God's being, maketh them all one
In Him, the Father, who are in the Son.

1849.

A DIRGE

ON THE SUBJECT OF A BEAUTIFUL POEM OF A FRIEND,*
IN THE GERMAN.

WITH a sweet smile the gentle features glisten,
Though noiseless death has frozen all below:
Unconsciously we stoop the head, to listen
For words that from these open lips should flow.
Along her brow the smooth, dark hair is
braided;
The yielding drapery folds smoothly round:
And on her breast there lies, but newly faded,
A token that the hand of love has found,
A lily of the vale,
Tender and slight and pale,
And in the bosom of its dark leaf shaded.

This form is mute! the soul that filled its being
Taught it to weep, to triumph, and to pray,
Gave it a skill of loving, hearing, seeing, —
She that was all to it, — is gone away.

* Dr. J. L. Tellkampf, member of the Upper House of the Germanic representative body of 1848.

This will not speak, but, silent and forsaken,
It only waits to be restored to dust
From which for a short moment it was taken:
Bright time! but it has passed, as all time must.
This sweet and pleasant smile
That lingers here a while,
It is the last that fellowship will waken.

So still it is, there seems to float before us
A slight strain, — that sweet voice we longed
to hear:
Her glad companions in her better chorus
Pardoning the love that bids her linger near;
And while in soft and tender words she singeth
What, last, those dear lips stood apart to say
(As one that back, with gentle motion bringeth
Some slight web that the wind had borne away)
They give their sister-aid,
And o'er the soul conveyed
The melody round every feeling clingeth:

"Weep not for one soon called to travel yonder
Ere she loved earth and things of earth too well:
Who in this weary wilderness would wander
Whom Christ had called in His fair house to
dwell?

Give ye these relics to the earth's calm keeping;
And let her share them to the grass and flowers,
With a new freshness all this cast form steeping
And filling up, with newer life, its powers.
No longer I am bound
In that close, narrow round;
Let smiles break up this darkness of your weeping."

The strain is hushed: it was but fancy speaking;
Yet may such higher sense be often mine!
For what in earth is better worth the seeking
From our good God, than such a boon divine,
To walk, as near the unseen confines rounding
This life of ours from that of spirits blest,
And hear sweet sounds across the limits bounding,
Sounds that wake feelings holiest and best;
As one that on the shore
Hears fitfully sweep o'er
The music from some happy isle resounding?

Sweet girl! thou hadst the poet-glance, that throweth
Its own bright hues where'er it chance to fall;
As the stained glass with mellow beauties streweth

All its glance toucheth, giving life to all.
Thou knewest, too, the frequent, holy feeling
That like some gentle creature, in his play,
Across thy quiet mind came silent stealing, —
Thou fearedst to move, lest he should start
away:
The gentle thought of thee
Shall in my heart be free,
Stirring new thoughts and finer ties revealing.

Schenectady, N. Y., 1841.

A BURIAL-HYMN.

TO BE SUNG ON THE WAY TO THE GRAVE.

We bring Thee, Lord, this little dust
  To lay in earth away:
In thy sure watch we meekly trust
  To keep it for the Day.

Thy will be done! This dust, all dead,
  Must lose its fairer form,
And graces in the deep grave shed
  That almost yet are warm.

We thank Thee for the little while
  Our child lived here in love,
To glad a narrow place with smile
  As from Thy house above.

And more, oh! we must thank Thee more
  That dew of upper day
Baptized his earthly being o'er,
  And spirit hallowed clay.

TO GOD, MOST HIGH.

O MY Lord, I have but Thee;
Other friends are faint and few,
To myself I am not true;
Yet, my God, Thou lovest me.

I am poor and have no more
But Thy love within my heart;
Earth shall never tear apart
That which is my hidden store.

Many, many doubts and fears,
I have many pains and cares;
But Thou comest, at unawares,
And I see Thee through my tears.

I would never be my own,
Nor on friends my heart-strings twine;
I do seek to be but Thine,
And to love but Thee alone.

Jesus! while Thy cross I see,
Though my heart do bleed with woe,
By those blessed streams I know,
Blood of Thine was shed for me.

O my Lord! Be Thou my guide;
Let me hold Thee by the hand,
Then, in drear and barren land,
I will seek no friend beside.

January 7, 1848.

LOVE DISPOSED OF.

HERE goes Love! Now cut him clear,
A weight about his neck:
If he linger longer here,
Our ship will be a wreck.
Overboard! Overboard!
Down let him go!
In the deep he may sleep,
Where the corals grow.

He said he 'd woo the gentle breeze,
A bright tear in her eye;
But she was false or hard to please,
Or he has told a lie.
Overboard! Overboard!
Down in the sea
He may find a truer mind,
Where the mermaids be.

He sang us many a merry song
While the breeze was kind:

But he has been lamenting long
The falseness of the wind.
Overboard! Overboard!
Under the wave
Let him sing where smooth shells ring
In the ocean's cave.

He may struggle; he may weep;
We 'll be stern and cold;
His grief will find, within the deep,
More tears than can be told.
He has gone overboard!
We will float on;
We shall find a truer wind
Now that he is gone.

1839.

TO MY OLD PARISHIONERS.

ON WRITING A TALE OF NEWFOUNDLAND.*

THE parish-priest that hath his charge
Beside the stormy sea,
Where howling tempests stalk at large,
And many an iceberg, as a barge,
Moors where the shallows be;
Where winter's sky, with sudden gust,
Is traversed to and fro,
And storm-clouds, broken up as dust,
Fill earth all deep with snow,
Hath much to speak of hardy men
That face the wild sea-gale,
And loving hearts made dreary, when
The waiting eyes must fail,
That from the cliffs their far search strain
To see, slow-toiling home again,
The long-familiar sail
That shall not come; for it is tost
Like drifting weed above the lost,

* In verse; afterwards given over. See note at the end.

Who down and down, through soundless deep,
Have found a pathway, sheer and steep,
And at the foot shall lie and sleep,
While long the hamlet's tale
Lingers upon their unknown fate,
And, night by night, the fire burns late
In one sad, silent cot,
Where wife and children spread their hands
And cower above the wasting brands,
And the poor house-dog understands,
Why they that went come not.

Often when holy prayers are said
Beside a new-made grave,
Some mother waileth for *her* dead;
She never held his heavy head
And mother's tears upon it shed
Ere dust to dust she gave.
He lieth where no foot may tread,
No little ones may there be led,
Where long, lank ocean-weeds are spread,
Beneath the shifting wave.
Sometimes, before accustomed date,
A boat comes lonely back, —
No colors flaunt, in joyful state,
Above her silent track:

She bringeth not accustomed freight,
But laboreth with some strange weight:
The air is chill and desolate
That breathes around her way,
As from the iceberg, cold and lone,
A stern, far-reaching chill is thrown
Abroad upon the day.
The skipper, from the helm, looks on
With fixéd eye and visage wan,
And hath no word to say.
The neighbors, gathered on the beach,
Gaze wistfully; and, each to each,
Breaking long pauses in their speech,
Conjecture, as they may.
Some one has dreamed, within the night,
"The minister, in clothing white,
Beside a grave did stand,
With head all bare, as reading prayer,
He held his book in hand.
Dark mourners, bending low around,
Wetted with silent tears the ground
And the rough grave-pit scanned.
Over-against them, on the east,
Were angel-forms, whereof the least
Was glorious and grand.
And, at the words, one scattered dust,

With bright hand on the coffin's crust,
And forth a form as of the Just,
Went with them to their land."
The simple men, that hear this dream,
Ask revérent questions, for they deem
Such things, how strange soe'er they seem,
No matter for a smile.
Now say they, as the boat sweeps by,
"The skipper's eldest son doth lie
Coffined within her, for his eye
Looked spirit-like, erewhile."
Ay, ay! And it is even so!
Soon flits about the news of woe:
"When the. Lord's day comes round,
The long procession, sad and slow,
Mounting the churchyard hill shall go,
To lay the young man's body low,
In consecrated ground."

Such are full-frequent things with those
That dwell beside the sea:
Whose sails feel every wind that blows,
If fair or foul it be.
Dear patient fishermen! for you
Whom late I lived among,
My heart, that loved you, yearns anew,

And often pass before my view
The forms of old and young.
For love of you this tale I tell
Of things now long agone;
And as the dark and heavy swell
Of memory heaves on,
With wrecks of loves once builded well
As if to live for aye,
Ye may shed tears like those which fell
From him that wrote this lay,
And who again now says farewell!
As he will always pray.

February, 1848.

NOTE. As this piece has been very kindly written of by friendly pens, the reader may be willing to see the beginning (supposed to be told, years after, by the mother-in-law, who was one of those making up the family party, of that year, down to the Labrador Fishery) of the Tale of

JOHN HAYES'S LAST VOYAGE.

"With fishing-gear and equipage,
All waiting to be gone,
The "Foam-bird" lay beside the stage,
And pleasant days came on.
A sweet, bright June had just begun,
And through some open door,
The days came, bringing summer's sun,

Where all was bleak, before.
The winds went racing off the land,
And back, from off the sea;
And sweet smells streamed, on every hand,
From gool * and forest-tree, —
But there seems a mist my eyes before:
'Twas a sad voyage, that year, down to the Labradore!

" And farther out, upon the Bay,
The dark and steady flow
Of waves bore off, and far away,
Beyond where sight could go.
The southwest wind, out there, was fair;
Day after day it blew
On, on, and on, as there were
No other path it knew:
Our wind! and each man took large share
Of what was yet to do.

" From Spaniards-Bay to Port-de-Grave, —
Along the shore, along the wave, —
There stood a warm-like shimmering haze,
That minded one of by-gone days.

" Just there away, the schooner lay,
Where yonder schooners ride;
The livelong day, she seemed at play
With the image at her side." . . . .

[Then was to follow a true account, in verse, (for it is a true story,) of what the author had told of his " Ladford," in " The New Priest." John Hayes saw what is called his " visage," and was lost in the schooner, much as Ladford is described to have been.]

* Sheep's laurel.

THE TEMPTER AT THE SIDE.

SEEST thou the shadow dogging at thy feet,
Without the breath of any at thy side?
Lo! there is one whom thou shalt never meet
Though thou do travel earth, both long and
wide;
Never in lonely field, — in crowded street, —
In joy or grief: whatever thee betide,
To meet thee face to face, nowhere shall he
abide.
Seest thou it at thy feet?
Know'st thou him at thy side?

He has been nigh thee since thy tottering pace
First faltered, doubtful, from thy mother's hand;
Anigh thee, yet, he hath his constant place,
Now that with strong men thou hast taken stand.
Go as thou wilt, thou winnest not the race;
Stay where thou wilt, in this or farthest land,
Untired he leaves thee not, whose face thou
hast not scanned.

He ever hath his place:
Ever is he at hand.

Albeit in the growing time of night
When the green things are starting everywhere,
And bud and leaf, sure of its tiny right,
Stretches towards its God for its blest share,
Then on thy longing mind celestial might
Has lighted down, and with quick vigor there
Has settled deep and still, — yet, not the less,
    beware!
Not present to thy sight,
The dark one loitered there.

Albeit in the stir and throng of men,
Catching warm influence from the glance of eye,
And thrill of words, that full and frequent, then,
Go kindling to the heart, ere they will die,
Thou hast not slumbered, — nor been coward,
    when,
If need were, thy lone voice must rise on high,
And thou go lone through all, — yet then that
    One was nigh,
Amid the crowd of men
On thee he kept his eye.

Albeit in the home's dear sunny scene,
Where low and homelike sounds, of birds and bees,
Float ever, streaming through that sea of sheen.
And wide peace bounds the world's strange haunts from these:
In that, — man's noblest place, — thy soul has been
Like a blest soul, familiar and at ease,
Sharing a heavenly love that sin could never seize,
He was in that pure scene,
Though thou wast all at ease.

Bethink thee how thy well-kept heart has known
Quick-starting thoughts, a frightful, poisonous growth;
Bethink thee how suggestions not thine own
Have crept and overcome it, slow and loth;
How a foul breath, o'er its bright vision blown,
Has buried all in the thick fog of sloth:
Dost thou not know him, yet, tempter and sharer, both?
He all thy moods has known,
When willing and when loth.

God set that shadow dogging at thy feet,
To warn thee one was ever at thy side
Whate'er thy state, to pour in promptings meet
From heavenly guided life to draw thee wide.
Therefore by day that shade doth near thee fleet,
Nor in the night that shadow is denied
When for God's light of day man's light has
been supplied:
Dark shadow at thy feet,
Dark foe is at thy side.

November 3 and 4, 1847.

A RHYME READ BY TWO LOVERS.

THE earth, without, was dark and very still:
No loving moon leaned downwards from the
night
To draw forth, out of darkness, vale and hill,
And wooded town, and far stream glistening
white;
And with her patient, maiden-modest skill,
Set the whole silent scene before her sight;
And the near park
Was still and dark,
And night and stillness, more than all
Clung to the trees beside the wet house-wall.
No insect's hum, nor bat-wing's whirring stroke,
Nor sudden cry the night's thick stillness broke.

Cool through the casement came light evening
airs
From off the meadows wet with summer-rain:
At times a rain-drop, shaken unawares,

Dripped from its hold, held long, but held in
vain.
The gauzy curtain, flowered, slight and frail.
Swelled with the soft air, like a pleasure-sail;
And, in the room, a rich, soft radiance fell
From the high, shaded lamp, on graceful things
Which woman knows to choose and set so well
That from her mere warm touch a new grace
clings;
And now, in that most still of summer eves.
Within the circle of the lamp's mild glow,
A youth and maiden turned the pictured leaves
Of a fair book; their two heads bending so
That each hears how the other's young heart
heaves:
(Ah! think we of our own loves, long ago?)
Her wreathéd, glossy hair now brushed his
cheek;
Now their quick eyes, by one sure, common
thrill,
Rose toward each other's, and they did not
speak,
For strongest, quick-winged speech
Has never learned to reach
Where love's fair meaning looks from cloudless
height.

Then she first dropped her slow lids, strong and
meek,
And both turned to their task, as with one will;
For two like these, knowing that subtile might
Fills all their features to the utmost grace,
Fear to show this beside each other's sight;
Scarce themselves dare to read other's face;
For their deep lives have surely mined, below,
Each toward the other, through the wall between,
Which soon shall fall, at some slight, sudden
blow,
And one wide love be where two hearts have
been.
O dear young love! Young love most bright!
Thou fairest thing this earth can show!
Old eyes will moisten at the sight,
Old hearts will feel the once-known glow!

A comely lady sat apart;
It might be she was deep in thought;
It might be that her very heart
Must go with what her fingers wrought;
Never by any chance
Her calm, wise matron-glance
That happy scene of young love sought.

A child, as fresh as that night's breeze,
Bright as the gone day's light,
Holding her own book on her knees,
Beneath her fast-fixed sight,
With many a half-frayed golden curl,
Sat near the lovers' seat:
Through sudden leap and race and whirl,
Chasing some story fleet,
Or asking oft, with knitted brow,
The little-heeding lovers, how
The words and sense could meet.
Her little unripe heart recks less
Of their delicious silentness.

The maiden's father, too, whate'er
His stately thoughts or fancies were,
Seemed, by all senses save of sight,
(Unlike the mother, calm and wise,)
Drawn to that circle of the light
Where the two felt each other's eyes.
And so, in that most still of summer-eves,
The youth and maiden turned their pictured
leaves.

"Read to me here," she said, and laid her hand,
Her soft, warm hand, on his, to point him where:

"Of 'The Night's Guest,' that I may understand
Why there is pictured here a churchyard bare
With rounded graves and tombs within the wall
And the tall, shadowing yew-trees over all:
Why Death stands here, within this open door,
That the old man waits, wearily, before."
The youth glanced at the picture while she said
Her gentle words, — and longer, — and then
read: —

THE NIGHT'S GUEST.

In the evening, cold and dreary,
Knocketh one at hostel-door:
All the way looks dark before
As the way behind was weary.

"Host! Hast thou a chamber quiet?
I have come a weary way:
Fain would rest till early day,
Far from wicked din of riot."

"I have many a quiet chamber,
Out of reach of human call:
And upon the outer wall
Scented briar and cypress clamber."

"Quick! O Friend! I may not tarry,
I am all with toil forespent:
And my aching knees are bent
With the weary weight I carry."

Rough-voiced was the Host and surly,
Yet he spake in softened tone:
"Hast a load, and art alone?
Go not to thy rest so early."

"Host, I am with travel broken:
Slumber weigheth on my eyes:
Yet I take in courteous wise
What in courteous wise was spoken.

"Lo! the load, that doth me cumber,
'Tis but this my body's weight;
I have borne it far and late;
Now I long for restful slumber."

"Yet I give but friendly warning,"
Said the Host in softened tone;
"Why, then, wilt thou go alone,
Since thou goest at early morning?"

"Host! I go not hence unfriended,
I have comrades for the way.
Now no longer bid me stay;
Let this longsome day be ended."

"Yea! but I have chambers many,
  Meet for many a different guest;
One in hallowed bed hath rest,
  One lies down unblest of any."

"Not so far I come unshriven;
  Weeping sore I sought release:
To my soul was spoken peace;
  Pledges twain to me were given."

"Yet forgive me: though thou seekest,
  Weary, nought but welcome rest,
Take my warning, O my Guest,
  Prove those things whereof thou speakest.

"Art thou of the Holy number?
  Dost thou know the Blessed Lord?
Canst thou give the Holy Word?
  Thou in hallowed bed shalt slumber."

"I may claim by Holy Mother,
  For the Blood that stained the Tree;
And the Word she gave to me
  Is, The Cross: I know no other."

"Now no more I may deny thee;
  Chide me not, mine honored guest,
That I kept thee from thy rest;
  'Twas the King that bade me try thee.

"Waiteth now thy quiet chamber,
  Thou wilt lie in hallowed bed,
Cross's sign above thy head,
  O'er the wall shall roses clamber.

"Thou hast well those pledges taken —
  Be thy slumber calm and sweet,
Till at early day, thou greet
  Him whose voice shall thee awaken."

So with courteous word and gesture
  Went the host before his guest:
Lighted him to place of rest:
  Help'd him doff his soilèd vesture.

Laid him down in chamber quiet,
  He that came from weary way,
Resting until early day,
  Far from wicked din of riot.

The two were graver when the tale was done:
And then the maiden said, "The old are sad
When all dear things have fallen, one by one.
And the dim eyes see earth with shadows clad."
She spoke far-looking forward into thought
Where from the poet's hand the scene stood
    wrought. —
"We are not old," the young man answer made;

"Nor does the world, to us, yet wear its shade.
We look, with longing eyes,
Where our bright future lies,
A fair, fair field, with glistering glories wet.
And fame and power, to win, ere the long sun
be set!"
She quickly turned to him, from her far thought,
And with full eyes his flashing glances caught.
Then he recalled himself from that great part,
But wearing half its look upon his face:
"And love"— he murmured, down into her
heart.
Already floating tears in her bright eyes had
place:
"What earthly thing shall last? What earthly
thing shall last?"
She said, most sadly: "Still must we forecast?"
But her round tears brought forth his answer,
fast.
"How can this change, until this life be
changed?
How can it change, till life itself be changed?"
He said: "Love is the very inmost thing.
From our own being we must be estranged,
Ere time to this deep love a change can bring."
"If it be God's," her voice most kind and dear

Spoke back, "the world cannot be drear:"
And when they parted, wishing each "Good
night!"
"It must be God's," she said; and she was right.
Then their two loves met at each other's lip:
Can life be drear, before such fellowship?
Peace to thee, dear young love! Good night!
Good night!
For not till youth, and life, and death is o'er,
Shall this world's love, thus hallowed, be no
more.
But the short story of the tired Night's Guest
Tells how that love, at evening, goes to rest.

THE BRAVE OLD SHIP, THE ORIENT.*

Woe for the brave ship Orient!
Woe for the old ship Orient!
For in broad, broad light, and with land in
sight,
Where the waters bubbled white,
One great sharp shriek! One shudder of
affright! —
And —
down went the brave old ship, the Orient!

It was the fairest day in the merry month of
May,
And sleepiness had settled on the seas;
And we had our white sail set, high up, and
higher yet,
And our flag flashed and fluttered at its ease:
The Cross of St. George, that in mountain and
in gorge, —
On the hot and dusty plain, —

[* Perhaps some may read this poem into an allegory of the Church of England and that of the East.]

On the tiresome, trackless main, —
Conquering out, — conquering home again, —
Had flamed, the world over, on the breeze.
Ours was the far-famed Albion,
And she had her best look of might and
beauty on,
As she swept across the seas that day.
The wind was fair and soft, both alow and aloft,
And we wore the even hours away.

The steadying sun heaved up, as day drew on,
And there grew a long swell of the sea.
And, first in upper air, then under, everywhere,
From the topmost towering sail
Down, down to quarter-rail,
The wind began to breathe more free.
It was soon to breathe its last;
For a wild and bitter blast
Was the master of that stormy day to be.

"Ho! Hilloa! A sail!" was the topman's hail:
"A sail, hull-down upon our lee!"
Then with sea-glass to his eye,
And his gray locks blowing by,
The Admiral sought what she might be.
And from top, and from deck,

Was it ship? Was it wreck? A far-off, far-
off speck,
Of a sudden we found upon our lee.

On the round waters wide, floated no thing
beside,
But we and the stranger sail:
And a hazy sky, that threatened storm,
Came coating the heaven so blue and warm,
And ahead hung the portent of a gale;
A black bank hanging there
When the order came, to wear,
Was remembered, ever after, in the tale.

Across the long, slow swell
That scarcely rose and fell,
The wind began to blow out of the cloud;
And scarce an hour was gone ere the gale was
fairly on,
And through our strained rigging howled aloud.
Before the stormy wind, that was maddening
behind,
We gathered in our canvas farthest spread.
Black clouds had started out
From the heavens all about,
And the welkin grew all black overhead.

But though stronger and more strong
The fierce gale rushed along,
The stranger brought her old wind in her breast.
Up came the ship from the far-off sea,
And on with the strong wind's breath rushed we.
She grew to the eye, against the clouded sky,
And eagerly her points and gear we guessed.
As we made her out, at last,
She was maimed in spar and mast,
And she hugged the easy breeze for rest.

We could see the old wind fail
At the nearing of our gale;
We could see them lay their course with the
wind:
Still we neared and neared her fast,
Hurled on by our fierce blast,
With the seas tumbling headlong behind.
She had come out of some storm, and, in many
a busy swarm,
Her crew were refitting, as they might,
The wreck of upper spars
That had left their ugly scars,
As if the ship had come out of a fight.
We scanned her well, as we drifted by:
A strange old ship, with her poop built high,

And with quarter-galleries wide,
And a huge beaked prow, as no ships are
builded now,
And carvings all strange, beside.
A Byzantine bark, and a ship of name and
mark
Long years and generations ago;
Ere any mast or yard of ours was growing
hard
With the seasoning of long Norwegian snow.
She was the brave old Orient,
The old imperial Orient,
Brought down from times afar
Not such as our ships are,
But unchanged in hull and unchanged in spar,
Since mighty ships of war were builded so.

Down her old black side poured the water in
a tide,
As they toiled to get the better of a leak:
We had got a signal set in the shrouds,
And our men through the storm looked on in
crowds:
But for wind, we were near enough to speak.
It seemed her sea and sky were in times long,
long gone by,

That we read in winter-evens about;
As if to other stars
She had reared her old-world spars,
And her hull had kept an old-time ocean out.
We saw no signal fly, and her men scarce lifted
eye,
But toiled at the work that was to do;
It warmed our English blood
When, across the stormy flood,
We saw the old ship and her crew.
The glories and the memories of other days
agone
Seemed clinging to the old ship, as in storm
she labored on.
The old ship Orient!
The brave, imperial Orient!

All that stormy night through, our ship was
lying-to,
Whenever we could keep her to the wind;
But late in the next day we gained a quiet
bay,
For the tempest had left us far behind.
So before the sunny town
Went our anchors splashing down;
Our sails we hung all out to the sun;

While airs from off the steep
Came playing at bo-peep
With our canvas, hour by hour, in their fun.
We leaned on boom or rail with many a lazy
tale
Of the work of the storm that had died;
And watched, with idle eyes,
Our floats, like summer flies,
Riding lazily about the ship's side.
Suddenly they cried, from the other deck,
That the Orient was gone to wreck!
That her hull lay high on a broken shore,
And the brave old ship would float no more.
But we heard a sadder tale, ere the night came on,
And a truer tale, of the ship that was gone.
They had seen from the height,
As she came from yester-night,
While the sea was running high,
And the storm not all gone by,
A ship driving heavily to land;
A strange great ship, (so she seemed to be
While she tumbled and rolled on the far-off sea,
And strange when she toiled, near at hand,)
But some ship of mark and fame,
Though crippled, then, and lame,
And that could not but be gallantly manned.

So she came, driving fast;
They could tell her men, at last;
There were harbors down the coast on her lee;
When, strangely, she broached to, —
Then, with her gallant crew,
Went headlong down into the sea.

That was the Orient;
The brave old Orient:
Such a ship as never more will be.

1857 and 1860.

SONGS OF OUR HOLY WAR.

O dear Lord, we know what death is worth:
Thou diedst in woe and pain upon the cross:
Out of thy death man's freedom had its birth,
And for his gain Thou gavest all thy loss.

HYMN FOR THE HOST IN WAR.*

WITH banners fluttering forth on high,
  And music's stirring breath,
Lord God! we stand beneath Thine eye,
  Arrayed for work of death.

When we our stormy battle wage,
  Thy Spirit be our zeal!
In conquering, teach us not man's rage,
  But Thine own ruth to feel.

Thy Christ led forth no host to fight,
  But He disbanded none:
And our true life, and our best right,
  By death alone He won.

Dear Lord! if we our lives must give,
  And give our share of earth,

* "Christmas" (Handel's), or any other solemn and stirring "Common Metre" tune.

To save, for those that after live,
  What makes our land's true worth,

Lead Thou our march to war's worst lot,
  As to a peace-time feast;
Grant, only, that our souls be not
  Without Christ's Life released!

O God of heaven's most glorious host!
  To Thee this hymn we raise;
To Father, Son, and Holy Ghost,
  One God, one voice of praise!

July 15, 1861.

NEW ENGLAND ARMING.

I.

Along the soil whereon we tread,
  Our fathers' prints are hollow:
The grass is taller where they bled;
  We will not fear to follow:
We have not less to love than they;
  Our hearts are not the colder:
Nor shall our sons, of younger day,
  With shame recall the older.

II.

We bear upon our muster-roll
  Such names as live in story;
And many more, that on that scroll
  Shall win their share in glory.
There were plain names at Bunker Hill,
  And modest answers met them:
Now, proudly known, we call them still:
  Can they that wear, forget them?

III.

Our home, our own old home, is dear
  By ties we cannot number:
The spoiler shall not trample here,
  Or death shall be his slumber.
But ye that taught her soil to bloom,
  And with fond toil have cherished,
Her flowers shall wave above your tomb
  If for her sake ye perished.

IV.

Here first arose the trembling cry
  Of freedom, feebly spoken:
Here last her lofty tones shall die
  When her proud heart is broken.
At Concord, and at Lexington,
  Our fathers stood for justice:
The fight was lost, the cause was won;
  In their own God our trust is.

V.

At every hearth some cherished form
  A lonely watch is keeping:
Our maidens see the rushing storm,
  And gentle eyes are weeping.

THE MASSACHUSETTS LINE.

Air: "*Yankee Doodle.*" *

I.

STILL first, as long and long ago,
  Let Massachusetts muster;
Give her the post right next the foe;
  Be sure that you may trust her.
She was the first to give her blood
  For freedom and for honor:
She trod her soil to crimson mud;
  God's blessing be upon her!

II.

She never faltered yet for right,
  Nor ever will hereafter;

* If the writer's dear native Commonwealth take this for her own, he begs for it no better and no other tune than "Yankee Doodle." Until we can reclaim from triviality the best and the only historical air that we have, — an air which, in slower time and with expression, can not only stir the blood, but draw the tears of one who has the truer sense, — we shall never have national melodies.

Fling up her name with all your might,
 Shake roof-tree and shake rafter.
But of old deeds she need not brag,
 How she broke sword and fetter;
Fling out again the old striped flag!
 She'll do yet more and better.

III.

In peace her sails fleck all the seas,
 Her mills shake every river;
And where are scenes so fair as these
 God and her true hands give her?
Her claim in war who seek to rob?
 All others come in later —
Her's first it is to front the Mob,
 The Tyrant and the Traitor.

IV.

God bless, God bless the glorious State!
 Let her have way to battle!
She'll go where batteries crash with fate,
 Or where thick rifles rattle.
Give her the Right and let her try,
 And then, who can, may press her;
She'll go straight on, or she will die;
 God bless her! and God bless her!

Duanesburgh, May 7, 1861.

It shall not be a coward's name
  That those loved lips are calling;
And never shall the tears of shame
  Fall where those tears are falling.

VI.

A secret prayer is rising there
  In timid accents given:
Our battle-cry shall fill the air
  And echo high in heaven.
Together we will fight and fall,
  Or we will live together:
One heaven shall bend above us all
  In storm or sunny weather.

1839: retouched, 1861.

THE MEN OF THE CUMBERLAND.

[This ship went down on the 9th of March, under Lieutenant George M. Morris, with her flag flying, and her guns firing (while the water was closing over them) at the iron monster "Virginia," which had cut two yawning holes in her side. The chaplain and one hundred and twenty of the crew are said to have sunk in her.]

CHEER! cheer! for our noble Yankee tars,
That fought the ship Cumberland!
And bare the head for their maims and scars,
And their dead that lie off the strand!

Who whines of the ghastly gash and wound,
Or the horrible deaths of war?
Where, where should a brave man's death be found?
And what is a true heart for?

Thank God for these men! Ah! they knew when

Was the time for true hearts to die!
How their flag sank, apeak, will flush the brave cheek
While this earth shall hang in the sky!

In the bubbling waves they fired their last,
Where sputtered the burning wad:
And fast at their post, as their guns were fast,
Went a hundred and more before God.

Not a man of all but had stood to be shot,
(So the flag might fly,) or to drown;
The sea saved some, for it came to their lot,
And some with their ship went down.

Then cheer for these men! they want not gold;
But give them their ship once more,
And the flag that yet hangs in wet and cold
By their dead at that faithless shore.

Our sunken ship we 'll yet weigh up,
And we 'll raise our deep-drowned brave,
If we drain those Roads till a baby's cup
May puddle their last shoal wave.

And we 'll tell in tale, and sing in song,
  How the Cumberland was fought
By men who knew that all else was wrong
  But to die when a sailor ought.

March 20, 1862.

NEW ORLEANS WON BACK.

A LAY FOR OUR SAILORS.

[The opening words of the burden are a scrap of old song caught up.]

Catch — Oh, up in the morning, up in the morning,
Up in the morning early!
There lay the town that our guns looked down,
With its streets all dark and surly.

God made three youths to walk unscathed
In the furnace seven times hot;
And when smoky flames our squadron bathed,
Amid horrors of shell and shot,
Then, too, it was God that brought them through
That death-crowded thoroughfare:
So now, at six bells, the church pennons flew,
And the crews went all to prayer.
Thank God! Thank God! our men won the fight,
Against forts, and fleet, and flame:

Thank God! they have given our flag its right
In a town that brought it shame.
Oh, up in the morning, up in the morning,
Up in the morning early!
Our flag hung there, in the fresh, still air,
With smoke floating soft and curly.

Ten days for the deep ships at the bar;
Six days for the mortar fleet,
That battered the great forts from afar;
And then, to that deadly street!
A flash! Our strong ships snapped the boom,
To the fire-rafts and the forts,
To crush and crash, and flash and gloom,
And iron beaks fumbling their ports.
From the dark came the raft, in flame and smoke;
In the dark came the iron beak;
But our sailors' hearts were stouter than oak,
And the false foe's iron weak.
Oh, up in the morning, up in the morning,
Up in the morning early!

Before they knew, they had burst
safe through,
And left the forts, grim and burly.
Though it be brute's work, not man's, to tear
Live limbs like slivered wood;
Yet, to dare, and to stand, and to take death
for share,
Are as much as the angels could.
Our men towed the blazing rafts ashore;
They battered the great rams down;
Scarce a wreck floated where was a fleet before,
When our ships came up to the town.
There were miles of batteries yet to be dared,
But they quenched these all, as in play;
Then, with their yards squared, and their guns'
mouths bared,
They held the great town at bay.
Oh, up in the morning, up in the
morning,
Up in the morning early!
Our stout ships came through shell,
shot, and flame,
But the town will not always be
surly;

For this Crescent City takes to its breast
The Father of Waters' tide;
And here shall the wealth of our world, in the
West,
Meet wealth of the world beside:
Here the date-palm and the olive find
A near and equal sun;
And a hundred broad, deep rivers wind
To the summer-sea in one:
Hear the Fall steals all old Winter's ice,
And the Spring steals all his snow;
While he but smiles at their artifice,
And lets his own nature go.
Oh, up in the morning, up in the
morning,
Up in the morning early!
May that flag float here till the earth's
last year,
With the lake mists, fair and pearly.

Duanesburgh, May 27, 1862.

A CALL OF TRUE MEN.

Up to battle! Up to battle!
All we love is saved or lost!
Workshop's hum and wayside's tattle,
Off! This thing the life may cost.
Come, for your country! For all dear things, come!
Come to the roll of the rallying drum!

You have seen the spring-swollen river
Hurling torrent, ice and wreck:
You have felt the strong pier quiver
Like a tempest-shaken deck: —
Many a stout heart, quick hand, and eye,
Broke the water's mad strength, and it went by.

Look on this mad, threatening torrent,
Tumbling on, with blood and death!
Will we see our bulwarks war-rent?
Never! Snatch a stronger breath:

Here is good man's work! Break through, and
through!
What matters hardship, or danger, to you?

What were death to any true man
If the cause be true and high?
Beastly might quails under human
Looking calmly in its eye.
Come! with your fearless strength break yonder
ranks!
God's blessing! glory! and evermore thanks!

August 5, 1862.

THIS DAY, COUNTRYMEN.

COWARDS, slink away!
But who scorns to see the foe
Deal our land all shame and woe,
Must come forth, to-day!

Crops are safe, afield;
Cripples and old men can reap.
Young and strong and bold must leap
Other tools to wield.

Cast the daily trade!
Never may be bought or won,
After this great fight is done,
What, To-day, is weighed.

Leave the true-love's side!
Go, be fearless and be strong:
Woman glories to belong,
Where she looks with pride.

True men hold our line:
Basely leave their true ranks thin,
Waste and ruin will rush in,
Like the trampling swine.

Who dares be a man?
Now, for home and law and right,
Go, in God's name, to the fight!
Rescue! while we can.

August 5, 1862.

MY TOWNSMEN FOR THE WAR.

A FIFE's shrill strain comes up the way;
Quick drum-beats make the pulses play;
Light sprays are waving overhead;
I hear a manifold tramp and tread:

Ah! you are soldiers, now, my kindly neighbors,
Learning the step and drill and watch at night;
Bound to that field where bayonets and sabres
Cut living flesh, and honest work is fight.

God bless you, there, as in this homely tillage!
One while, our brow's sweat, — one while, heart's red gore.
Keep safe the free homes! save the land from pillage!
Give to some right, once, — peace to all, once more!

We must be ready for our Time to call us;
Noble and brave, the best have answered first:

We must be men, let good or ill befall us :
Self-slaves and cowards in their blood are curst.

What has God set us in His living world for,
Save for the work that falls upon our day?
His iron smites the bosom it was hurled for,
One in his honest place, and one, away.

Go your great way! the sight of you has
kindled
Awe for a simple man's undaunted will :
Men of great place, and men's great gains, have
dwindled :
Daring of death for right grows higher still.

Soldiers, keep near best thoughts of homes that
bred you :
Love, and the Prayer, and Parent's kind re-
proof ;
Toil and earned rest ; the maiden that shall
wed you ;
Plenty and peace beneath the farmer's roof.

Think of our Road, and Hill, and far-seen
Churches ;
Neighbors that gather on the Sabbath-morn ;

Hear the harsh cry from where the peacock
perches,*
Not breaking that strong peace, of God's Word
born.

Think of our God, by whom your pledge is
holden;
Do your work well: He sees it from above:
So, by and by, along the streets all golden,
March in blest triumph under eyes of love!

The fife's shrill strain faints far away:
Again bright stillness holds the day.
The drum's dull sound, behind the hill,
Lets down the blood's warm, hurried thrill.

It is not like our full-ripe grain
To cut fellow-men down, made in vain:
But come they crushing truth and right,
Sinks their low manhood out of sight.
By manful hands God fells man's crime:
The way shows forth: we see the time.

To some of us no high call comes
To march with clarions, flags, and drums,

* These simple reminders will touch our townsmen's hearts.

And fling our life-strength into the throng:—
We have our prayer and speech and song.
Some take a place: the great Fate glides,
Far angels peering from the sides;
And farther down are won the gains,
Safe law, broad right, and broken chains.

Duanesburgh, July, 1863.

THE FAILURE AT FREDERICKSBURG,

UNDER THAT TRUE MAN AND SOLDIER, MAJOR-GENERAL BURNSIDE.

WAS nothing gained? Is this not gain, so high
A mark for us and after-comers set?
Life is at strongest that can greatly die,
And manhood better worth than all men get.

Is this not gain, that our slow, flabby heart,
Dull-laboring, long, in sordid work and trade,
With quick, strong, throb thrown back to it should start,
And learn that beat wherewith great deeds are made?

At need best blood may better far be shed
Than frame fair thought, or drive the wheel and plough:
No fathers yet for country nobly bled,
Whose sons are not the nobler livers now.

To push the bridge up to the flaming guns,
To throng the rocking skiffs, in death's broad sight,

To wade the trench where their own life-blood
runs, —
This was to conquer, if they lost they fight.

They fail not, that their face still forward keep,
And lift their stout hearts up from every
fall :
They fail that in mid-stream dread greater
deep ;
They fail, that, losing little, fear for all.

Here in far home, by safe ties tamely held,
We shame to write of these things brave and
high,
Though our own blood from its next veins has
welled,
And meekly we dare hope that we could
die.

But shall your great deeds want their written
fame ;
Our coward voices give you back no cheer ?
To sit aghast or dumb were greater shame
Than thus to warm to manhood, even here.

January 8, 1863.

PRAYER IN THE FIGHT.

[From KÖRNER, 1831, revised 1846.]

FATHER, I call on Thee!
Roaring, the smoke of the battle rolls o'er me;
Flashing, the lightning of death is before me:
God of the battle, I call on Thee:
Father, oh, lead Thou me!

Father, oh, lead Thou me!
Whether to conquer or perish betide me,
Lord, Thy commandment ever shall guide me.
Lord, as Thou will, so guide Thou me:
God, I acknowledge Thee!

God, I acknowledge Thee!
As when the leaves in harvest-time rustle,
So in the war-tempest's terrible justle,
Outspring of Grace, I acknowledge Thee.
Father, oh, bless Thou me!

Father, oh, bless Thou me!
Life I commit to Thy hands, in heaven ·

Well mayest Thou take what by Thee has
 been given:
 In living, in dying, bless Thou me!
 God, I give praise to Thee!

God, I give praise to Thee!
Strife is not here for mean barter or chattel;
All that is holiest hangs on our battle:
 Fall we, or stand, I give praise to Thee:
 God, I submit to Thee!

God, I submit to Thee!
When me the thunder of death has greeted,
When from my veins the life's-blood has fleeted,
 To Thee,—I commit myself to Thee:
 Father, I call on Thee!

OUR LAND BEYOND THE WAR.

When our good God shall give us rest from
fighting,
And send our soldiers singing from the field,
Where the great wrong has found its bloody
righting
From men that life, but never right would yield ;

There, in long peace, when sunny plenty hovers,
With sounds of mirth and work, o'er all the
land,
There homelike households are, and sly, true-
lovers,
And merry children, gambol, hand in hand ;

Brailing their sails, the pennoned ships, deep-
freighted,
Come sliding through the ranks of anchored
hulls ;
In stony streets, the roar of trade belated,
Touches almost the morrow ere its lulls ;

Over the world to thee, shall lowly dwellers,
Look, lovingly, Free Land, as fondly we;
And at dim hearths, and in dark ways, the
tellers
Of thy proud fame and thy great hope shall
be.

1863.

www.ingramcontent.com/pod-product-compliance
Lightning Source LLC
LaVergne TN
LVHW011213110826
845150LV00006B/1417

* 9 7 8 1 4 2 5 5 1 7 5 7 1 *